The Macat Library
世界思想宝库钥匙丛书

解析约翰·A. 霍布森
《帝国主义》

AN ANALYSIS OF
JOHN A. HOBSON'S
IMPERIALISM: A STUDY

Riley Quinn ◎ 著
黄辉辉 ◎ 译

上海外语教育出版社
SHANGHAI FOREIGN LANGUAGE EDUCATION PRESS

目 录

引 言 ………………………………………………… 1
   约翰·A. 霍布森其人   2
   《帝国主义》的主要内容   3
   《帝国主义》的学术价值   5

第一部分：学术渊源 ………………………………… 7
   1. 作者生平与历史背景   8
   2. 学术背景   12
   3. 主导命题   17
   4. 作者贡献   21

第二部分：学术思想 ………………………………… 25
   5. 思想主脉   26
   6. 思想支脉   31
   7. 历史成就   36
   8. 著作地位   40

第三部分：学术影响 ………………………………… 45
   9. 最初反响   46
   10. 后续争议   50
   11. 当代印迹   55
   12. 未来展望   60

术语表 ……………………………………………… 65
人名表 ……………………………………………… 70

CONTENTS

WAYS IN TO THE TEXT	77
Who Was John Hobson?	78
What Does *Imperialism* Say?	79
Why Does *Imperialism* Matter?	81
SECTION 1: INFLUENCES	85
Module 1: The Author and the Historical Context	86
Module 2: Academic Context	91
Module 3: The Problem	96
Module 4: The Author's Contribution	101
SECTION 2: IDEAS	105
Module 5: Main Ideas	106
Module 6: Secondary Ideas	111
Module 7: Achievement	117
Module 8: Place in the Author's Work	122
SECTION 3: IMPACT	127
Module 9: The First Responses	128
Module 10: The Evolving Debate	133
Module 11: Impact and Influence Today	139
Module 12: Where Next?	145
Glossary of Terms	151
People Mentioned in the Text	156
Works Cited	160

引 言

要 点

- 约翰·A. 霍布森（1858—1940）是英国经济学家和政治思想家。
- 《帝国主义》一书出版于 1902 年，该书提出国际侵略往往是由国内经济状况所导致。
- 霍布森是最早提出不平等性与侵略性外交政策之间存在直接联系的学者之一。他进一步指出两者之间的这种联系与富人阶层和政治团体所施加的不当影响有关。这种关联性无论是在当下还是在 19 世纪的英国都持续存在。

约翰·A. 霍布森其人

《帝国主义》(1902) 的作者约翰·A. 霍布森 1858 年出生在英国德比郡，1940 年去世。曾在牛津大学主攻古典文学，即古希腊与拉丁文学，毕业后开始其记者生涯。霍布森全家都从事报刊业，他的父亲还在德比郡创办了一份报刊。霍布森曾为《曼彻斯特卫报》（该报于 1959 年更名为《卫报》，至今仍享誉全球）撰稿。他在《曼彻斯特卫报》担任的最重要的工作之一就是对布尔战争*进行报道，布尔战争是发生在英国与荷兰移民后裔之间的一场冲突，交战地点位于今天的南非。

作为一名公共知识分子，霍布森是伦敦多家知名"伦理"俱乐部的成员，与创办伦敦政治经济学院（伦敦的一所知名学府）的社会主义*团体费边社*常有来往。霍布森一边参加这些社团聚会，一边为一些自由主义*周刊撰稿，此类周刊在自由和社会正义等问题上的政治观点与霍布森一致。霍布森在非洲南部的经历以及他在伦理社团所担任的工作对他后来在《帝国主义》一书中的核心观点产生了重要影响。霍布森不仅是一位自由主义思想家，也是一位颇具名望的经济学家。他与好友阿尔伯特·马默里*（一名商人和登山运动员）合著了《工业生理学》一书，该书是针对当时很多经济理论的重要批评论著。

霍布森目睹了第一次世界大战*期间欧洲列国如何从争霸世界演变为互相开战，因此他对人性的看法也多了些个人视角，少了些经济学视角；而作为欧洲公共知识分子的经历，则最终使他对人性产生了怀疑。

《帝国主义》的主要内容

霍布森在《帝国主义》一书中试图回答一个主要问题：帝国主义外交政策（即以缔造帝国为目的的外交政策）背后的逻辑是什么？

当时的普遍共识是，征服他国领土会扩大贸易，故能使所有人从中获利——总结成一句话就是"贸易跟着国旗走"。霍布森对这种观点提出质疑，认为占领新的土地并不会对贸易产生影响；由于维持大英帝国需要高昂的财力与人力成本，他试图从其他方面来解释帝国主义计划实施的动因。

霍布森认为帝国确实能带来经济利益，但获利的只是极少数富有资本家（粗略来讲，也就是投资者与企业主）。他是完全从经济学角度得出这个结论的。

霍布森与好友马默里共同提出了"过度储蓄"理论，该理论指出个别群体存在为自己过多储蓄的行为。由于这些钱没有通过再投资进入经济流通环节，越来越多的钱都被搁置在银行储蓄账户中。二人据此推论，由于许多穷人买不起工厂生产的产品，所以富人们不会把钱投资在工厂之类的地方。于是，他们把钱投资于海外矿产和铁路等。但是，霍布森指出，由于世界上大多地方并不像英国那样安全，于是富人们便会利用他们的政治关系来推进帝国主义政策。

霍布森认为，如果财富可以重新分配，那么国内的穷人手中就会有足够的钱，这样富人就能将钱投资在国内获得利润，而不必去寻求国外市场。他将这种重新分配称作"社会改良"，并将其建立在"社会自由主义"*——即国家机构应该保障公民的自由——的理念之上。这种观点强调社会群体有过上富裕生活的权利，政府应确保他们的需求得到满足；如果政府政策只能使极少数人受益，那么它就是极不民主的，而且也会严重损害英国普通民众的利益。

该观点还包含了另一个重要问题，即通过操纵他国领土来获取经济利益的帝国主义*政策的道德问题。

即使帝国主义的经济依据不成立，人们依然试图为帝国主义辩护，认为欧洲人有义务去"教化野蛮人"，并以此作为帝国主义得以合理存在的道德依据。霍布森指出这些论断仅仅是为了掩饰帝国的经济野心，并进一步指明了帝国主义者在教化的过程中实施操控的路径。这也指出了"殖民化"（文明社会享有的权利被扩展到其他领土）与"帝国化"（一个群体被他国的另一个群体所剥削）的显著不同。

帝国主义不仅会给附属国带来问题；在霍布森看来，帝国主义政策同样也会对英国文化产生危害。他认为帝国主义使英国社会愈加好战——士兵们一贯接受的训练就是要表现出一种强悍的态度，通过暴力而非对话来解决问题。这样一来，所谓的好士兵并不一定是一位好公民。霍布森认为，那些在帝国中学会统治本领的政治家们往往比在英国学会统治本领的政治家们更有可能去压制本国公民。

《帝国主义》的学术价值

根据霍布森的观点，"金融家"*——也就是依赖投资而谋生的人——在帝国主义计划中施加了一定的影响，而这似乎与他们的身份不太相称。不过，霍布森并没有详细解释这些金融家到底指的是谁。此外，我们可以这样认为，霍布森对资本主义*与帝国主义之间的界限划分过于明确，令人产生质疑。因此，对于学生们来说，该书提供了一个极佳的案例研究。其中的推理虽然有趣，但却过于简单，或许没有考虑到现实世界的复杂性。

尽管霍布森的理论不被大多数同行所接纳，但马克思主义*学者却对他的理论甚为关注，并赋予了它重要地位。那些受经济学家、社会主义理论家卡尔·马克思*理论影响而进行社会分析的学者都认同霍布森的观点，即资本主义（一种现今在西方及多数发展中国家占据主导地位的经济体制）必定会滋生帝国主义。不过，与霍布森不同的是，他们认为解决问题的途径在于革命而非改良。

在20世纪，霍布森对帝国的批判一直影响着许多政治思想家，不过现今帝国主义政策的批评家们与霍布森却极少有相似之处。例如，霍布森探讨了一群狭义概念上的投资者在实施帝国主义罪行中所扮演的角色，而美国文学理论家、哲学家迈克尔·哈特*与马克思主义哲学家安东尼奥·内格里*等政治哲学家和思想家却认为帝国主义只是一种"心态"。对他们而言，帝国主义这一概念定义了世界上所有的社会关系——这种观点极大地扩展了该术语的使用范围及内涵。

而且，现代读者可能会对霍布森关于帝国主义的道德合理性观点持怀疑态度；比如，霍布森认为当帝国主义在促进"文明传播"时是合乎道德的。这种说法暗示着不同社会之间存在优劣之分，现在已不再有说服力了。

虽然霍布森的一些观点已经过时，然而其理论所指明的整体方向却仍然相当重要。从更广泛的角度来看，《帝国主义》探讨了经济与政治问题的关联性。政治家与金融家联手就可以重塑世界从而达到他们的目的——尽管霍布森的论证并没有完全证明这一点，但是他的论点的确启发了一代学者。在20世纪众多追随霍布森步伐的最重要的理论家中，有许多都是马克思主义者，他们关注帝国主义何以改头换面而持续存在。霍布森的论断能够给学生提供一种新的视角来理解强权国家如何在冷战*（1947—1991年间苏联及其阵营与美国及其阵营之间的僵持局势）时期扩大影响范围。

此外，《帝国主义》一书还可以帮助读者学会质疑那些为外国侵略辩护的托词；虽然霍布森的著作未能提供一套完整的理论来解释帝国主义政策缘何产生，但它至少能够让我们明白政治论断是如何扭曲现实，使它变得模棱两可而无法判断。

第一部分：学术渊源

1 作者生平与历史背景

要点

- 《帝国主义》一书具有重要的研究价值,因为它从道德与经济学角度对国际侵略的经济依据进行了分析。
- 霍布森是许多左翼组织的成员,同时担任一些左翼报纸的记者,曾对布尔战争(英国试图从荷兰移民后裔布尔人手中夺取对现今南非绝大部分领土的控制而发动的战争)进行过专题报道。
- 19 世纪,欧洲国家都加入了对外国领土的"争夺战"。

为何要读这部著作?

英国经济学家、激进主义*改革者约翰·A.霍布森在 1902 年出版的《帝国主义》一书中提出,帝国主义——在他国领土进行"缔造帝国"的政策——无论是对英国国内还是对英国附属国而言都是一种消极力量。"激进主义"一词在此处指的是致力于通过社会改革来捍卫社会正义的英国左翼政治传统。

霍布森的此部论著与其他反帝国主义论著的显著区别在于它是从伦理与经济视角展开论述。霍布森不仅谴责帝国主义政策的非道德性,同时揭示了它有损帝国绝大多数公民的福祉。

当时流行的观点是"贸易跟着国旗走"(意思是英国的帝国扩张也意味着英国贸易基地的扩张,据称此举可提高每个人的生活水平)。[1] 不过,霍布森却持不同观点。他认为帝国主义旨在保护海外的主要资本投资,以牺牲纳税人的利益为代价,为极其富有的金融家这群"寄生虫"阶层谋福利。[2] "资本投资"在这里指的是用于投资产生利润的金钱——这也是金融家们赖以生存的手段。

霍布森称自己是一名"异端经济学家",其思想的原创性值得人们铭记。《帝国主义》也不例外。英国政治学家杰里米·科尔宾*在 2011 版《帝国主义》的引言中写道,"那时候的争议在于他分析了一个国家在篡夺新的帝国属地过程中所面临的巨大压力。"[3]

> "值得关注的是霍布森能够区分商业利益与帝国主义目标的不同,并对二者进行拆解分析。他证明了其他欧洲国家即使没有从帝国中获利,也都成功地以各种手段跃居成为贸易与工业强国。"
>
> —— 杰里米·科尔宾:《帝国主义》"引言"

作者生平

霍布森于 1858 年出生在英国德比郡一个中产阶级家庭。他的父亲是一位富有的报业老板。1876 年,他进入牛津大学学习,主攻古典文学(古希腊与拉丁文学),并在学习之余对哲学与政治经济学*(经济学的一个分支,主要研究政治如何影响实体经济效益)产生了浓厚兴趣。

回到伦敦后,霍布森做过记者与讲师;后来,他被派驻如今的南非去报道布尔战争,即 1899—1902 年间发生在大英帝国与荷兰移民后裔布尔人之间的一场冲突。作为一名记者与公共知识分子,霍布森颇为多产,撰写了许多短篇与文章。事实上,《帝国主义》一书主要由这些文章汇编而成。这些文章"大都撰写于 1901 至 1902 年间,一些发表在重量级的学术刊物上,但是大多数都发表在像《讲述者》这类较为随意的自由主义与激进主义周刊上"。⁴"自由主义"在这里指的是英国政治中强调个人自由重要性的一股思潮。

这些文章都是霍布森于布尔战争刚刚结束时在伦敦创作的。非洲的所见所闻深深地影响了霍布森，也使他更加确信帝国主义是极少数富人阶层强加于多数民众身上的一种可怕的计谋。⁵霍布森圈子内的大多数人都是伦敦"伦理社团"的资深会员。这些左翼知识分子会定期会面并探讨社会主义政治、哲学与经济问题。

创作背景

整体而言，《帝国主义》一书所处时代最重要的历史特征是"晚期"英帝国主义——又被称作"非洲争夺战"*时期——具体而言，指的是布尔战争时期。19世纪90年代，欧洲列强都醉心于从非洲掠夺土地；剑桥历史学家约翰·朗斯代尔*将这场争夺战比作一场赛马比赛："一群越野赛马闯进了非洲腹地"，并注意到"欧洲如何从先前的霸权主导地位强势转变为"一种直接的政治操控。⁶

资深帝国主义列强（英国和法国）与帝国计划的新加盟者（比利时、德国和意大利）之间的竞争导致了非洲政治局势的巨大改变。有学者指出，"1879年，（非洲）大陆90%以上都被非洲人所统治，"但是到了1900年，也就是霍布森创作《帝国主义》的时期，"除了一小部分之外，非洲绝大部分地区都被欧洲列强所操控。"⁷

霍布森之所以对欧洲争夺非洲这一时期如此关注，主要是因为他曾担任《曼彻斯特卫报》的通讯记者，对布尔战争做过报道。英国记者、作家和左翼知识分子纳撒尼尔·迈尔*写道："英国一直以来都成功地征服了移民人口，并且对南非盛产矿藏的地区施加政治上与经济上的操控。但是，这场战役囚禁了许多农村妇女和儿童,可以说是一次令人耻辱的溃败,这促使了许多热心人士对英国的政治体制进行反思。"[8]

不过,早在那些领导者扪心自问之前,霍布森就在探寻他们的政治与经济动机。

---

1. 约翰·霍布森:《帝国主义》,诺丁汉:斯伯克斯曼出版社,2011年,第65页。
2. 霍布森:《帝国主义》,第85页。
3. 杰里米·科尔宾:《帝国主义》"引言",约翰·霍布森著,诺丁汉:斯伯克斯曼出版社,2011年,第7页。
4. P. J. 凯恩:《霍布森与帝国主义:激进主义、新自由主义和金融:1887—1938》,牛津:牛津大学出版社,2002年,第82页。
5. 凯恩:《霍布森与帝国主义》,第92页。
6. 约翰·朗斯代尔:"非洲历史上的欧洲争夺与征服",载《剑桥非洲历史:1870年—1905年》(第六卷),罗兰·奥利弗与 G. N. 桑德逊编,剑桥:剑桥大学出版社,1985年,第681页。
7. 罗兰·奥利弗和安东尼·阿特莫尔:《1800年后的非洲》,剑桥:剑桥大学出版社,2005年,第118页。
8. 纳撒尼尔·迈尔:"引言",载《帝国主义》,约翰·霍布森著,诺丁汉:斯伯克斯曼出版社,2011年,第15页。

2 学术背景

要点

- 政治经济学的主要学术研究领域关注财富的本质,以及社会如何走向繁荣富裕。

- 虽然以亚当·斯密*和杰里米·边沁*为代表的自由主义政治经济学家(即主张个人自由的经济思想家)都认为帝国主义从经济角度来讲成本高昂,但是约翰·斯图尔特·密尔*等却认为其价值在于"教化"荒蛮之地。

- 虽然霍布森认为市场通常都是不完善的,但他认同古典自由主义思想家的观点,也就是帝国主义——主要以获利为目的夺取他国领土的政策——不仅成本高昂,也是不道德的。

著作语境

约翰·A.霍布森的《帝国主义》是一部政治经济学著作。根据英国政治哲学家约翰·斯图尔特·密尔的著名定义,政治经济学这一学术传统主要关注"财富的本质以及财富生产和流通的法则,这些也直接或间接地包含了人类社会走向繁荣或没落的原因机制。"[1]

换句话说,政治经济学考察财富与社会的关系,以及不同的财富生产方式如何能促进或阻碍社会繁荣。从密尔的论断中可以得出的一个重要结论就是,政治经济学领域主要关注"如何分配及生产最大价值"的哲学及思想。因此,政治经济学是一个比纯粹的政治学或经济学更为"宽广"的学科领域。

霍布森深受政治经济学领域自由主义传统的影响。自由主义传统强调个人自由，认为社会应该走向"理性"。该传统的形成在很大程度上要追溯到英国著名的政治理论家约翰·洛克*。约翰·洛克在论著《政府论·下篇》中提出政府的职能就是要保护私有财产，² 该部著作被公认为自由主义思想的奠基之作。自由主义政治经济学家一贯保持着批判帝国主义的传统；如果政府的职能仅仅是保护人们的权利和财产，那么维持帝国运转就在其职能之外，因而就是浪费时间与金钱。

> "在人类生活的方方面面，实践远远早于科学……因此，政治经济学作为一门科学的诞生是现代以来的事，但是它所探究的主题一直以来都与人类主要现实利益挂钩，在某些时期尤其得到人们的关注。这个主题就是财富。"
> —— 约翰·斯图尔特·密尔：《政治经济学原理》

学科概览

霍布森深受一些广为接受的自由主义概念的影响，这些概念是由自由主义的核心思想家（尤其是苏格兰经济学家亚当·斯密、英国哲学家与社会改良者杰里米·边沁和英国政治哲学家约翰·斯图尔特·密尔）提出的。

自由主义与帝国主义从一开始就关系紧张。斯密在其代表性论著《国富论》中强调了帝国奉行重商主义*（粗略来讲，指的是政府对贸易的鼓励政策）所付出的巨大代价。他写道，虽然帝国"（培育了）一个消费者国度，消费者不得不从不同商家商铺购买产品……但是，国内消费者一直都承担着维持和捍卫帝国的巨额成本",而这对他们非常不利。³ 边沁在1793年撰写的题为《解放殖民地》的册子中提及了帝国主义的道德问题。"(放弃)你们的殖民地吧,"他敦促欧洲政治家,"因为你们没有权利统治他们,因为他们不愿受你们统治。"⁴

相比而言,密尔提出帝国主义应被视为英国与属地之间的一种互利关系,而该观点使传统的自由主义立场愈加复杂。密尔和稍晚一些的霍布森一样,都认为英国存在人口与资本(大意指可用于投资的钱)过剩,因此需要借助帝国向国外寻求一个出口。但是,和霍布森不同的是,密尔认为帝国是一个好的解决办法,并声称大英帝国不仅将英国的自由主义思想传播到世界上所谓的"无人居住"的土地上,而且"未开化的属地也受益于英国所提供的秩序与安全、投资与贸易"。⁵

尽管这些思想家在观点上存在分歧,但他们都关注社会繁荣与道德之间的关系。在许多方面,反对帝国主义政策的政治经济学观点通常都认为帝国主义政策是毫无价值、成本高昂且无利可图的,而且从权利角度来看是不道德的。密尔对帝国主义的辩护仍属于这种思路,只是他认为"教化"帝国属民这一行为的道德性可以证明帝国主义是合理的。

学术渊源

霍布森的自由主义思想可追溯到他在牛津大学的经历。在牛津大学读书时,霍布森结识了自由主义思想家T. H. 格林*。受格林的影响,霍布森将自己的立场大致定义为一种"新的"*(或"社会的")自由主义⁶:也就是说,他认为国家在确保个人自由方面发挥一定的作用,其主要职责就是确保经济与社会公正。

格林关于"消极"自由与"积极"自由差异的讨论尤其出名。"消极"自由是一种不受限制的自由，如言论自由。"积极"自由指被赋予某种能力（比如学会发表言论）。⁷ 这是"古典"自由主义与"新"自由主义的一个重要区别：古典自由主义强调不受政府干预的自由（消极自由），而新自由主义强调个体帮助他人的义务。

与霍布森同时代的批评家 P. J. 凯恩* 写道，新自由主义认为个人存在缺陷，因此强调团体而非个人的权利。这使新自由主义者拒绝接受萨伊定律*关于完美市场机制的说法。根据萨伊定律，生产是所有需求的源头——也就是说，一个工人会用他或她的个人收入购买产品，这反过来又会刺激其他领域的生产。

相反，新自由主义者认为市场"会带来分裂，加剧贫困，甚至导致社会分崩离析"，因此市场需要政府的积极调控。⁸ 这一观点也得到了 19 世纪另外两位著名的自由主义者约翰·拉斯金*和理查德·科布登*的大致认同。他们两位对霍布森的影响很大，霍布森甚至着手撰写了两人的传记。

科布登是最早也是最尖锐地指出帝国主义对英国不利的学者之一。他写道："我脑海中一直坚信我们在印度的事业是不可能实现的，而且也是无望的。"⁹ 霍布森将对帝国的传统自由主义分析——帝国代价高昂且不道德——又推进了一步。他坚持认为帝国主义计划不仅是一种错位的民族狂热，还是金融家（给企业提供巨额贷款并从中获利的人）的一项盘算已久的计划。

1. 约翰·斯图尔特·密尔:《政治经济学原理》,伦敦:朗曼出版社,1865年,第1页。
2. 约翰·洛克:《政府论·下篇》,C.B.麦克皮森编,印第安纳州印第安纳波利斯:哈克特出版社,1980年,第20页。
3. 亚当·斯密:《国富论》,伦敦:迪吉瑞兹出版社,2009年,第391页。
4. 杰里米·边沁:转引自伯纳德·波特《帝国批判者:英国激进主义者与帝国主义的挑战》,伦敦:I.B.特瑞斯出版社,2007年,第8页。
5. 艾琳·沙利文:"自由主义与帝国主义:J.S.密尔的大英帝国之辩",《思想史杂志》第44卷,1983年第4期,第607—609页。
6. P.J.凯恩:《霍布森与帝国主义:激进主义、新自由主义和金融:1887—1938》,牛津:牛津大学出版社,2002年,第21页。
7. T.H.格林:"自由立法与契约自由",载《T.H.格林政治理论选集》,约翰·R.罗德曼编,纽约:美瑞迪斯出版社,1964年,第44—45页。
8. 凯恩:《霍布森与帝国主义》,第21页。
9. 理查德·科布登:转引自波特《帝国批判者》,第13页。

3 主导命题

要点

- 《帝国主义》的核心问题是:"帝国主义外交政策背后的经济根据是什么?"
- 该争论并非一场学术争论,而更多地是一场公众争论;政治圈内外的人士都试图证明帝国主义的商业依据("贸易跟着国旗走")与道德依据("我们有义务对野蛮人进行教化")是合理的。
- 霍布森与其自由主义同僚反对这些观点。霍布森的反对论点是基于一套非常缜密的科学理论。

核心问题

随着欧洲列强非洲争夺战的拉开,许多政治经济学家都开始思考这样一个问题,"这种帝国主义外交政策背后的经济根据是什么?"最常见的关于帝国主义经济学的解释是由重商主义者提出的:他们坚持认为"贸易跟着国旗走"。重商主义的基本观点就是帝国需要大量原材料来满足国内工业生产,因此需要在国外扩张领土。原因有两个:第一,这些领土能够提供国内生产产品(可能是衣服、家具和枪支等)所需的原料;第二,这些产品一旦加工出来,就会被输出到最初提供原材料的殖民地,以供殖民地人民购买。该观点强调一个国家与其属地之间存在最兴旺发达的贸易关系,这意味着帝国主义对宗主国来说,是一种可行且合乎情理的经济政策。

该观点遭到了质疑,这不难理解。包括亚当·斯密和霍布森在内的许多自由主义思想家都认为重商主义模式存在极大缺陷,并且英国实际上要为帝国主义付出巨大代价。大英帝国与17世纪荷兰移民者后裔在现今南非所爆发的布尔战争，在很大程度上就是该问题的体现，尤其需要记得的是霍布森曾亲眼目睹这场溃败。霍布森看到了帝国主义显而易见的荒谬性，在书中他试图思考英国为何会醉心于这样一个错误的冒险。在谈论英国的这场争斗时，以金融资本主义*——即通过私人投资获得的私人利益——的狭隘利益之名犯下的错误被遮掩了起来。因此，霍布森等人对帝国主义政策的经济与道德依据提出了质疑。

> "这场战争（布尔战争）对于每个英国人和南非人来讲都是一场可怕的灾难，但是对于矿主来说却意味着由于矿区集约化生产与投机运营所带来的巨大的利润增长。"
>
> ——约翰·霍布森：《南非战争》

参与者

就霍布森而言，这场在帝国主义支持派与反对派之间展开的争辩并没有像现代学术界的争论一样在期刊或大学校园内展开，而是采取高度公开的形式，在新闻界以及各政治党派之间进行。

大多数主战派报纸的观点又有所不同。正如一位历史学家所说的那样："伦敦记者倾向于将布尔人描绘成原始、落后的形象……通常用动物特性对他们加以描述……因此他们被英国这样文明先进的国家所击败是社会达尔文主义*的必然结果。"这大致证明了胜利者内在的优越性与"进化"的高级性。[1] 国内论场上则弥漫着一种极端爱国主义*，那些批判布尔战争的人都被讥讽为"亲布尔派"或"反英派"；霍布森认为这场争论的性质接近于"沙文主义"*

（他指的是一种极端的爱国主义）。他的这些经历被收录在《南非战争》一书中。²

但这并不是一场简单的公开辩论。霍布森是自由党*的成员。自由党试图建立一个基本的福利国家和一个更加世俗化的社会，并将个人自由置于习俗与传统之上。但是英国国会中的自由党成员却在帝国主义问题上存在分歧；那些同情布尔人的自由党人虽然并没有形成任何领导组织，却不约而同地谴责"英国在布尔战争中动用的军事手段是完全没有必要且有悖人性的"，尤其在建立集中营*这一做法上。而那些主战派自由党人往往忽略这些问题，他们认为"帝国主义是大家都争先恐后想骑的一匹马"。³ 由于这场争论不是在学术圈而是在政治领域展开的，因此随之而来的是一些微妙的妥协。人们没有再深究帝国主义的根源，而这场论辩的参与者们则对如何推进教条主义的看法、人道主义事业以及自己的政治生涯更感兴趣。

当时的论战

霍布森所采用的方法与国会中自由党同僚的方法有很大不同。霍布森属于激进派（即主张通过社会改革来进一步实现左翼自由主义的目标），他拒绝接受人们对帝国主义的普遍看法，认为帝国主义既是不道德的，也要付出无谓的高昂代价。但是，霍布森绝不是唯一一个对帝国主义进行批判的激进分子，也不是唯一一个指控金融家是帝国主义的主要煽动者的学者。例如，霍布森的好友、苏格兰激进派记者 J. M. 罗伯逊写道："（帝国主义的）首要目标不是去购买产品，而是去销售产品，得到货物作为报偿后，再去开始新一轮的销售；其最终目标是积累更多用于投资的资本。"⁴ 这些攻击进一步印证了反帝国主义是一项自由主义事业。但略有不同的是，霍布森越来越关注金融资本主义。尽管与霍布森同时代的许多人（罗伯逊是其中之一）都认为工业是帝国主义的核心，但霍布森却将矛头指向一个特定的群体，认为他们应负首要责任。[5]

这样看来，霍布森并不是简单地追随古典自由主义*思想家或新自由主义思想家。古典自由主义思想家支持自由贸易，仅仅从道德立场反对帝国主义，而新自由主义思想家则认为对市场进行干预是合乎道德的，他们仅仅指责金融家过度储蓄的反社会性行为是在某种程度上鼓励帝国主义计划。

相反，霍布森创建了一套社会科学理论并得出了许多经得起验证的结论。这套理论构建了以投资为目的的资本主义与帝国主义之间的直接关联——这对反帝国主义事业的思想观点是一项重大贡献。

---

1. 肯尼斯·摩根："布尔战争与媒体"，《20世纪英国史》第13卷，2002年第1期，第5页。
2. 约翰·霍布森：《南非战争：起源与后果》，伦敦：詹姆斯·尼斯贝特有限公司，1900年，第228页。
3. 约翰·奥尔德："自由主义的亲布尔派"，《英国研究》第14卷，1975年第2期，第93—94页。
4. J. M. 罗伯逊：《爱国主义与帝国》，伦敦：格兰特·理查兹出版社，1900年，第172页。
5. 彼得·凯恩："激进主义、格莱斯顿与迪斯累里'帝国主义'的自由主义批判"，载《全球秩序的维多利亚视角：19世纪政治思想中的帝国与国际关系》，邓肯·贝尔编，剑桥：剑桥大学出版社，2007年，第226页。

4 作者贡献

要点

- 霍布森认为帝国主义是金融资本主义——即以私人利益为目标的私人投资——的直接产物,并且国内的不平等导致了国外帝国主义。
- 《帝国主义》试图否定"帝国主义是有利可图的"这一观点,并进一步提出帝国主义是国内不平等状况的必然结果。
- 该论断是基于"消费不足"理论*。该理论认为对产品或服务的需求不足会导致国家经济的停滞不前。

作者目标

霍布森认为英国的帝国主义政策是少数超级富有的金融家阶层的一个阴谋,并对之进行了极为猛烈的批判,这促使《帝国主义》一书从类似著作中脱颖而出。换句话说,帝国主义是资本主义的产物。

霍布森认为帝国主义是由国内经济政策导致的,[1] 他的目标是提供一套严密、科学的理论来解释英国社会存在的极度不平等为何会导致其在国外推行帝国主义政策。他认为这个政策只是迎合少数精英阶层的利益:"金融家"已经积累了大量的资本,以至于他们无法再在英国进行有利可图的投资,因此需要借助军事力量来保障其在国外的投资(比如金矿与铁路)。

霍布森在该书中竭力主张通过改变政策来远离帝国主义——他认为帝国主义意味着政府被这些金融家所绑架;他倡议推行累进税

制*（税收与收入相关联）、提高最低工资标准及实行国内再分配方案等社会改革措施，从而确保国内过剩资本（可用于投资的利润）以工资形式掌握在国内消费者手中。² 尤为重要的是，霍布森试图唤醒的不仅仅是英国公众的正义感（虽然他明确指出帝国主义的不道德性）。他希望向民众揭示富有资本家阶层是如何欺骗他们的，以及反对帝国主义对民众自身是极为有利的。

> "仅仅对帝国主义或军国主义*进行攻击，将它们视为政治上的权宜之计或政策都是白费力气的，唯有将斧头砍向这棵树的经济根基，并且切断帝国主义所为之效劳的阶层通过此途径所获得的剩余利润。"
>
> ——约翰·霍布森：《帝国主义》

研究方法

为了说服读者，霍布森除了反对帝国主义的经济根据、揭示金融家是如何推行一种有损于他人利益的政策之外，还运用了其他论述方法。《帝国主义》的独特之处在于霍布森将英国国内财富分配不均的现象与在国外推行的帝国主义政策联系起来，从而揭示两者的直接因果关系。他的理论极具价值，因为它不仅是在进行道德说教，而且得出了许多经得起检验的预测。也就是说，霍布森的理论预测到一个国家的金融资本家阶层最终会促使该国政府推行帝国主义政策——这只不过是一个时间早晚的问题。

这个极其大胆的预测也是削弱霍布森理论可信度的主要原因之一。

霍布森的观点是建立在他提出的一个经济理论之上，他在与商业人士阿尔伯特·马默里合著的《工业生理学》(1889)一书中提出了这一理论。这就是"消费不足"理论。

正统经济学认为生产与消费总是大致持平的,但是霍布森却认为这种观点扭曲了事实。霍布森写道:"如果按需对收入或消费力进行分配的做法是可行的,那么显而易见,随着生产力的每一次提升,消费也会同时增加。"但事实并非如此;生产增加与消费增长并不匹配,因为金融资本家已经积累和囤积了大量财富,以至于大多数消费者缺少资金来进行大量消费。由此而引发的消费不足又会促使金融家在国外寻求有效利用资本的途径。[3] 他们需要建立一个帝国来将资金投入其中,从而赚取利润。

时代贡献

霍布森在1898年的论文《自由贸易与外交政策》中首次将帝国主义政策与消费不足联系起来。他写道:"虽然英国生产的所有'商品'在国内具有潜在的市场,但却并没有'有效'需求。"[4]

这里,他试图描述这样一种情形:消费者有购买商品的欲望,但资本家的过度储蓄阻碍了消费者的购买力,使得货币无法进入流通环节,而大量囤积在资本家手中。

富人们"没有这种欲望",因为他们只需花费一小部分钱就可以满足"他们的物质需求",而那些"有消费欲望的人们却没有购买能力"。[5] 换句话说,由于经济不平衡,富人们手中的钱多到可以满足他们最奢侈的欲望,而穷人们却没有办法赚取足够的钱来满足他们最基本的需求。

霍布森与马默里在《工业生理学》中写道:"储蓄会增加现有的资本总量,(但是)同时也会减少实物与服务的消费数量。"任何

"过度"储蓄都会使过多的资本流入少数资本家手中,这样既降低了资本的价值,也使普通民众手中没有资金用于消费。[6]

---

1. 约翰·霍布森:《帝国主义》,诺丁汉:斯伯克斯曼出版社,2011年,第112页。
2. 霍布森:《帝国主义》,第108页。
3. 霍布森:《帝国主义》,第105页。
4. 约翰·霍布森:"自由贸易与外交政策",转引自约翰·D.卡宁汉姆·伍德和罗伯特·D.伍德《约翰·A.霍布森:著名经济学家的批判性评价》,伦敦:劳特利奇出版社,2003年,第XXXV页。
5. 霍布森:转引自伍德和伍德《约翰·A.霍布森》,第XXXV页。
6. 阿尔伯特·马默里和约翰·霍布森:《工业生理学:论现有经济学理论的某些谬论》,伦敦:约翰·默里出版社,1889年,第VI—VII页。

第二部分：学术思想

5 思想主脉

要点 🗝

- 霍布森研究的核心主题包括富人阶层的政治影响力、"消费不足"导致的经济停滞及其后果,以及如何通过社会改革来解决这些问题。

- 霍布森的核心论点是:消费与生产并不总是持平的,因为金融资本主义导致了消费不足,进而打破了两者之间的平衡;金融资本家利用这种不平衡进行海外资本投资并加以稳固;帝国主义可通过"社会改革"得到遏制。

- 霍布森论证的不足之处在于结构欠周密,且对其理论体系中占据重要地位的"金融家"的定义过于宽泛。

核心主题

约翰·A.霍布森的1902年著作《帝国主义》在整体上提出了一个极具争议性的观点:某些社会特殊利益群体——这里指的是金融资本家——有权力指使英国推行帝国主义政策。对霍布森而言,富有的金融资本家是"帝国引擎的发动者",因为他拥有"推进帝国主义(为之服务的)进程所应具备的权力集中以及精明的算计能力"。[1]

该结论是基于包括霍布森的消费不足理论在内的一系列支撑性论据而得出的。消费不足理论主要由三个相关联的观点组成:

- 富人阶层的过度储蓄导致了工业经济中资本的供应过量(粗略来说,也就是如果富人更喜欢储蓄而不是投资或消费,那么他们手中的钱就会囤积在那里而不产生任何价值)。

- 这反过来为富人向国外输出资本创造了强大的动力。
- 资本输出这一目标又促使他们去影响外交政策的制定。

霍布森认为,"社会改革"是消除帝国主义的根本所在;财富的公平分配会消除由于消费不足而导致的不平等,从而打消富人夺取海外土地的念头。

霍布森认为,尽管人们是理性的,但是如果他们想做最有利于自己的事情,那么就难免会犯错,因为他们很容易受到迷惑而不清楚哪些东西真正对他们有利。这一观点是霍布森的社会自由主义思想的核心所在。作为一种政治哲学,社会自由主义主张政府需要通过社会改革来重新分配资源,从而确保所有人都能获利。

> "并不是工业的发展要求开拓新的市场和投资领域,而是消费力的分布不均阻碍了一个国家内部商品与资本的消费。"
>
> ——约翰·霍布森:《帝国主义》

思想探究

霍布森论著中最重要的观点就是,金融资本主义不仅助长了帝国主义,而且直接催生了帝国主义:"帝国主义形成的原因在于工业的主要操纵者力图扩大其剩余财富流动的渠道,通过寻求国外市场与国外投资,来输出他们在国内不能销售或使用的商品与资本。"[2]

对于霍布森而言,这种状况的根源就是"国内资本的不合理分配。(金融家阶层对资本的)过度储蓄是帝国主义得以产生的经济根源，而这种过度储蓄项目包括租金、垄断利润及其他非劳动收入或额外收入。"[3]

更重要的是，这些囤积起来的资本在国内毫无用处；虽然这些资本金额巨大，但它们大多数不在实际消费者手中。霍布森认为，如果最初就不允许这些超级富人们积累这么多资本的话，那么"争夺国外市场或国外投资领域"的需求就会消失。[4]

该观点尤其值得关注，因为它使萨伊定律更加复杂化。萨伊定律是以法国自由主义经济学家让-巴蒂斯特·萨伊*的名字命名的。该定律提出，在一个持续的经济周期中，商品生产者在获得报酬后会去购买其他人生产的产品。但是正如霍布森所见，过度储蓄会使萨伊定律失效；那时就需要政府干预来维持消费与生产之间的平衡，从而确保经济活动处于一种自然、有序的状态。

霍布森针对这个问题提出的解决办法并不是放弃帝国主义：这样只能治标不治本。相反，霍布森建议废除不受监管的资本主义，这是帝国主义最初得以产生的根源。他的解决方案就是通过社会工程或社会改革来实现财富的重新分配。通过社会改革，导致英国资本供应过剩的国内不平等问题就会得到解决，并且金融家阶层推进帝国主义的巨大动因就会得到遏制。工会*（保护工人阶级利益的劳动者协会）和社会主义（粗略来讲，是一种主张政府应对自由市场进行干预从而保证社会财富合理公平分配的政治哲学）作为社会改革的两大引擎，"是帝国主义的天敌，因为它们从'帝国主义'阶层那里夺回了构成帝国主义经济基础的剩余收入。"[5]换句话说，只有正视由国内经济状况而引发的帝国主义问题，英国的外交政策才可能变得合乎道德。

语言表述

这部作品的一个主导命题——金融家的过度储蓄致使他们不得不借助帝国主义来进一步实现自身利益——在该书的第一部分已经得到了清晰的阐述。霍布森在论述前通常以图表的形式清晰地呈现数据，然后直入主题。尽管如此，他在表达观点时仍有两个方面做得不尽如人意。

首先，霍布森的整体理论是建立在一个假设之上，但是他并没有对该假设进行充分的论证或探讨：他认为金融家阶层有一种近乎完美的能力去引导由"政治家、士兵、慈善家和商人"构成的"爱国主义力量"去支持一种帝国主义政策，而这一政策并不为大众谋利。[6]但是，霍布森并没有阐释清楚这些富有的大人物是如何对政府施加控制的。

其次，该书的后半部分并没有向读者解释清楚金融家究竟是引领了帝国主义潮流，还是仅仅跟随国外政治扩张之风。他们要么是充分发挥"自身权力集中与精明算计的天分来推进帝国主义计划"，要么是"仅仅本能地依附着任何强烈、真实和崇高的感情……然后利用它来满足他们的目的"。[7]霍布森的论述显然是自相矛盾的，这使得读者很难判定究竟哪个策略占据了主导地位。

霍布森的核心观点遭到质疑的原因在于他在试图构建因果关系时，将金融家阶层视为一种分析手段的倾卸场：对于金融家阶层，他并没有给出清晰的定义，并且这一阶层似乎拥有无限的权力。这个问题使许多评论家将霍布森的著作斥为"阴谋论"。[8]

1. 约翰·霍布森:《帝国主义》,诺丁汉:斯伯克斯曼出版社,2011年,第88页。
2. 霍布森:《帝国主义》,第106页。
3. 霍布森:《帝国主义》,第107页。
4. 霍布森:《帝国主义》,第107页。
5. 霍布森:《帝国主义》,第110页。
6. 霍布森:《帝国主义》,第88页。
7. 霍布森:《帝国主义》,第88、191页。
8. 纳撒尼尔·迈尔:"引言",载《帝国主义》,约翰·霍布森著,诺丁汉:斯伯克斯曼出版社,2011年,第29页。

6 思想支脉

要点

- 霍布森对帝国主义的道德批判是基于以剥削为目的的"帝国主义"和以领土扩张为目的的"殖民主义"*之间的区别。他也警示了帝国主义可能会对国内民主造成威胁。

- 霍布森的次要观点驳斥了帝国主义在道德上的正义性,并且对帝国主义的经济后果没有过多提及;这涉及另外一场争论。

- 霍布森提出资本主义制度通过消除世界范围内的其他替代性制度来进行自我保护。该观点使人们重新审视霍布森的《帝国主义》一书。

其他思想

　　霍布森核心论点的主旨——国内的不平等现象导致了在国外推行帝国主义政策——在其更具有哲学性的支脉思想中得到了论证。霍布森竭力驳斥"帝国主义能为全球带来利益"这一观点,并警示极端军国主义——一种易于采取军事行为的社会倾向或基于军事模式构建的社会——可能会对英国国内局势造成影响。他认为,国外帝国主义的扩张意味着国内自由主义民主的缺失。

　　虽然"帝国主义"与"殖民主义"可能看起来内涵相同,但是霍布森却通过概述民族权利的扩张和权力的施行之间的差异,对这两个术语进行了重要区分。霍布森将民族主义*定义为"在民族性的基础上建立一个政治团体",所以殖民主义仅仅是通过将拥有完全政治权利的公民迁移至无人居住的地方来实现该政治团体——和民族——的扩张。另一方面,"当一个民族向民族边界之外的地方前进",并且不去统治拥有完全政治权利的本族公民而是暴力占有与剥削外国属地和人民的时候,帝国主义就诞生了。[1]

理解"殖民主义"与"帝国主义"的差异,对于领悟霍布森关于"英国的国际计划该如何实施"的道德论点至关重要。

> "一位好公民与一位好士兵在行为上存在着绝对对立。士兵的最终目的通常不是像一般所误认为的那样为国而战死,而是为国而杀戮。"
> ——约翰·霍布森:《帝国主义》

思想探究

在霍布森生活的时代,"教化使命"被视为帝国主义的道德目标。但是,霍布森在他的国际性论断中却反对这一观点。他写道:"在思考(帝国主义)干预的伦理与政治问题时,我们绝不能被评论家们宣扬的所谓'劳动尊严'和'教化使命'这些显而易见的骗人把戏所愚弄和蒙蔽。"[2] 霍布森认为,对"低等种族"唯一合法的干预就是帮助他们最终建立一个理性的自治政府,而不是为了文明国家的利益去剥削他们。[3]

这种将帝国主义视为对殖民地人民有益的一种教化的观点可以追溯到英国自由主义哲学家约翰·斯图尔特·密尔。密尔总结出社会发展的四个阶段:最初人类社会处于原始蒙昧状态,之后进入奴隶社会,"其主要特点是'智力'低下……以及'国民性格中的显著缺陷',从而不可能建立代议制政府";最后进入现代自由主义国家状态。[4] 他认为更为发达的国家必须鼓励那些落后国家进行发展。

但是，霍布森认为密尔总结出的四个阶段只是为了剥削所谓的"低等种族"并从中获利的一种道德托词。这样一来，"人们对'低等种族'就不会产生发自内心的同情，而这种同情对于施加最佳的教化具有至关重要的影响。"[5]

他也指出了帝国主义对国内的不利影响，认为帝国主义会助长军国主义，从而破坏国家内部的民主。霍布森写道："到目前为止，我都是从狭隘的经济角度来看待帝国主义的问题。然而，更为重要的是军国主义的政治影响，这关乎普遍自由与普通公民道德的根基。"[6] 因此，自由主义与军国主义是作为互相对立的原则而存在的，"前者的目的在于培养一名好公民，而后者则在于培养一名好士兵。"[7]

换句话说，好公民通常表现出一种友好、合作的态度，而好士兵则往往表现出一种独裁、强势的态度。霍布森认为，当一名士兵进入政府之后，他更可能习惯于发号施令、镇压民众。但是，这种将帝国主义计划视为自由主义的对立面而对其进行批判的观点并不是霍布森首创的。这种观点可以追溯到19世纪中叶的自由主义者，比如英国政治家理查德·科布登。科布登写道："这可能看似乌托邦，但是我并不同情那些大国或者那些通过疯狂扩张帝国来追求民族荣耀的人。我想看到的是个人的成长、发展与提升。"[8]

被忽视之处

霍布森著作的第二部分关注与帝国主义相关的政治问题。相较于第一部分对帝国主义经济依据的探讨，第二部分的内容所获关注甚少。不过，经济历史学家拉尔斯·马格努松*认为，目前人们开始对该书常被忽略的第二部分进行关注，这在很大程度上为霍布森的理论注入了新的生机。20世纪以来,大多数霍布森理论的阐释家与批评家都仅仅关注霍布森是如何从狭隘的经济角度对帝国主义进行阐释的,并习惯将《帝国主义》视为俄国革命领袖弗拉基米尔·列宁*所著的马克思主义分析论著《帝国主义是资本主义的最高阶段》一书的原型*。

但是,马格努松认为,我们有必要将经济阐释置于政治阐释的语境中展开,而通过这种方式就可以发现霍布森不仅仅是列宁的原型。他坚持认为霍布森对"1870年后的侵略性帝国主义"真实画面的勾勒依赖"(社会达尔文主义)理论的出现,包括种族理论以及强化的民族主义和未经正确引导的爱国主义思想的复兴"。[9]

换句话说,马格努松声称,如果用正确的方式去解读霍布森的著作,我们就会发现《帝国主义》的第二部分和第一部分具有同等分量,并且这种经济学角度的阐释只是包含历史、政治、意识形态和经济学在内的更为复杂的理论体系的一部分。

马格努松认为,以这种方式去看待霍布森对理解整部作品具有重要意义。对他而言,《帝国主义》"应该被视作现代制度经济学*的先驱"——制度经济学即研究制度与理念如何塑造经济行为的学科——"而不仅仅是列宁帝国主义*理论的原型"。[10]

马格努松还指出,霍布森理论中金融资本家所起的作用实际上是相对有限的,并且霍布森的帝国主义理论与美国经济学家托斯丹·凡勃伦*的观点更为接近。凡勃伦认为,"帝国主义只不过是王朝政治的更名换姓,其主要目的是满足未在场物主的利益而非未在场君主的利益。"[11]在马格努松对霍布森进行重新评估的语境中,不难发现霍布森与凡勃伦的观点具有明显相似之处。对霍布森而言,爱国主义与种族主义等机制起到了一个关键而非次要的作用,而凡勃伦将"爱国主义……视为其关于资本主义以及国际层面的帝国主义理论的一个额外的解释变量"。[12]

---

1. 约翰·霍布森：《帝国主义》，诺丁汉：斯伯克斯曼出版社，2011年，第45—48页。
2. 霍布森：《帝国主义》，第213页。
3. 霍布森：《帝国主义》，第214页。
4. 贝特·贾恩："康德、密尔和国际事务中的非自由主义遗产"，《国际组织》第59卷，2005年第1期，第194页。
5. 霍布森：《帝国主义》，第250页。
6. 霍布森：《帝国主义》，第142页。
7. 霍布森：《帝国主义》，第144页。
8. 理查德·科布登：转引自伯纳德·波特《帝国的批判者：英国激进主义者与帝国主义的挑战》，伦敦：I.B.特瑞斯出版社，2007年，第14页。
9. 拉尔斯·马格努松："评价霍布森与帝国主义"，载《五十年后再看J. A. 霍布森》，约翰·菲比编，伦敦：麦克米伦出版社，1994年，第156页。
10. 马格努松："评价霍布森与帝国主义"，第160页。
11. 托斯丹·凡勃伦：《遥领所有制与近代企业》，纽约：凯利出版社，1964年，第35页。
12. 斯蒂芬·爱德格和朱尔斯·汤申德："约翰·霍布森、托斯丹·凡勃伦与帝国主义现象：金融资本、爱国主义与战争"，《美国经济学与社会学杂志》第51卷，1992年第4期，第412页。

7 历史成就

要点

- 虽然霍布森关于帝国主义的"科学"理论本身并没有产生持久的影响,但是他思想体系的核心论点仍然具有重要意义。
- 帝国主义在20世纪一直持续存在,在对该现象的研究中,霍布森的著作仍具现实意义。
- 《帝国主义》和种族问题之间有着千丝万缕的联系:霍布森暗示犹太人参与了帝国主义计划。

观点评价

虽然《帝国主义》仍然占据重要地位,但是约翰·A.霍布森未能充分阐释不平等性与帝国主义之间的直接因果关系。霍布森在论述时很容易走向"概念性滑移",也就是说,他对帝国主义的分析似乎有些矛盾:对某些概念的论述时而狭义,时而广义。最明显的例子就是霍布森的"资本家是帝国主义的操纵者"这一观点,以及资本家是否相信他们自己的沙文主义(即对自己国家的一种极端的热爱)。

该书第一部分指出,帝国主义者都是一些见利忘义的金融家,他们只不过是受投资需求驱使,试图操纵轻信的英国政府去推行一种具有破坏性的帝国主义政策。[1] 但是,在该书后半部分,当霍布森探讨帝国主义所带来的心理影响时,他却将金融家阶层描绘成感情丰富的爱国主义者:"帝国主义政治家、军人或公司董事们都通过描绘非洲奴隶掠夺的残忍场面来推行一种扩张性政策。他们并不是故意或有意运用这些策略来煽动英国公众。他们仅仅是本能地表现出自己强烈、真实而高涨的情感……并利用它达到自己的目的。"²

如果说霍布森的论述没能引起人们对帝国主义政策的普遍质疑，这正是因为这种概念性滑移。虽然"金融家阶层"对他的理论而言极为关键，但是他对金融家阶层的定义却随着论述的展开而不断改变；不过，这可能是由于《帝国主义》在创作之时并不是一部完整的著作，而是由多篇论文拼凑而成。

> "但是，我们必须再次强调霍布森的持久贡献在于他对帝国主义的心理分析。霍布森极尽所能地揭示了人类具有的自我欺骗这种无尽潜质的根源。对于那些在国内普遍会受到谴责的政策，人们自然会寻求一些道德托词来说服民众支持它们。"
>
> —— 哈维·米切尔："再看霍布森"，《思想史杂志》

当时的成就

霍布森显然非常急切地想创建一套接近科学的普遍适用的帝国主义"理论"，但是他可能夸大了事实。他写道，国家财富的分配不均会导致全球帝国主义，就像火会产生烟一样，不过考虑到社会现实的复杂性，他的观点可能有些绝对。这也在很大程度上解释了为什么他的作品在自由主义思想家那里遭到了冷遇，甚至很快就被公众遗忘了。后来，人们对霍布森的理论逐渐产生了兴趣——最初俄国共产主义领袖弗拉基米尔·列宁的马克思主义思想受他影响，后来在20世纪60年代的冷战（美国及其同盟国与苏联＊及其同盟国之间长达44年的对峙局面）背景下，人们对帝国主义的研究又重新兴起。

帝国主义的焦点最初在英国,后来转移到美国,冷战时期则转向苏联。正如迈克尔·巴拉特·布朗*在《帝国主义经济学》一书的引言中所写的那样,对帝国主义研究的兴趣重燃"确实反映了人们对(关于帝国主义行为的)狭隘的政治阐释的普遍不满。比如,将美国长期以来在加勒比海及东南亚地区的行为解释为'捍卫世界自由'是无法令人信服的。"[3]

局限性

《帝国主义》因其反犹太主义*(反对犹太人的情绪)和欧洲中心主义*(将欧洲和欧洲人置于显著地位的观点)的倾向而一直遭到批评。

前者来自于霍布森的一种观点,他认为操控帝国主义政策的金融家阶层主要由"某个单一而特定的(犹太)种族的人构成,他们已积累了上百年的金融经验"。[4]在霍布森的政治圈内,反犹太主义情绪非常普遍。霍布森最终被视为一种固化思维模式的受害者,他惯于将"(布尔)战争的责任归咎于一些犹太金融家的不道德动机"。[5]

虽然霍布森指控犹太人要为资本主义负责,但这并不是他论点的主要构成部分,并且这种观点并没有影响今天人们对霍布森的看法。但是,他进一步将"低等种族"视为需要引导的儿童,这在现代语境中引发了许多争议。他认为白人对非白人社会的介入是一种必要的"教化使命",而这一结论构成了霍布森为一种"仁义的"或"理性的"帝国主义辩护的基础。[6]

加拿大国际关系教授戴维·朗*指出,霍布森勾勒的图景存在许多问题。首先，霍布森没能认识到，这些社会完全能够自治而无需白人的干涉。其次，霍布森认为帝国主义的问题"不在于对属地民众进行控制，而在于西方列国之间寻求控制权的竞争，而这是一个不称职的父亲或老师才会做的事情。"[7]这种批评思路使霍布森对一种"理性的"帝国主义的呼吁有些站不住脚，也进一步揭示出，虽然霍布森对资本主义的愿景是受到他所看到的社会不公正现象的启发，但这种愿景本身缺乏一种准确性。

---

1. 约翰·霍布森：《帝国主义》，诺丁汉：斯伯克斯曼出版社，2011年，第86页。
2. 霍布森：《帝国主义》，第191页。
3. 迈克尔·巴拉特·布朗：《帝国主义经济学》，伦敦：企鹅出版社，1974年，第17—18页。
4. 霍布森：《帝国主义》，第86页。
5. 哈维·米切尔："再看霍布森"，《思想史杂志》第26卷，1965年第3期，第400页。
6. 霍布森：《帝国主义》，第216页。
7. 戴维·朗："家长制与帝国主义的国际化：J. A. 霍布森论'低等种族'的国际政府"，载《国际关系领域的帝国主义与国际主义》，戴维·朗和布莱恩·施密特编，奥尔巴尼：纽约大学出版社，2005年，第87页。

8 著作地位

要点 🗝

- 霍布森的主要关注点是如何将经济理论与政治后果联系起来，不过他在后期主要关注的是政治。
- 霍布森后期的作品忽略了对帝国主义经济依据的探讨，而是更多地关注人性问题。
- 霍布森的作品在其有生之年并未受到重视；就连崇拜霍布森的经济学家约翰·梅纳德·凯恩斯*也认为霍布森的写作风格令人困惑，并且其作品质量也参差不齐。

定位

约翰·A.霍布森的《帝国主义》写于其多产的创作生涯中期。虽然这部作品通常（虽然不是唯一）被誉为他的不朽名作，但它既不是霍布森第一部关于经济学的主要论著，也不是他第一部关于帝国主义的论著。

霍布森的第一部重要著作是1889年与英国商人阿尔伯特·马默里合著的《工业生理学》一书。该书对消费不足理论进行了概述，而这一理论成为霍布森后期许多著作的主题。《帝国主义》并不是霍布森的第一部反帝国主义著作。他在1898年发表的《自由贸易与外交政策》一文中阐释了经济帝国主义理论，将消费不足理论与帝国扩张联系起来，并提出国内改革是一种和平、可取的替代办法。在该文中，他将帝国主义与实现财富均衡分配所需的"国内社会和工业改革"进行了严格区分。[1] 霍布森会在《帝国主义》一书中继续对该理论进行论证。

他最终修正了自己的极端立场，在其自传《一个异端经济学家的自白》中写道："我用上了我所有的战斗本能，来捍卫我的异端观点：资本主义是造成分配不公、过度储蓄以及冒险帝国主义的经济动力的根源。这一度导致我过于简单地宣扬历史的经济决定论。"² 霍布森在他的晚年（霍布森于1940年去世，即《一个异端经济学家的自白》出版两年后）对帝国主义采取了一种更为宽泛的看法：他认为帝国主义是由人性中的贪婪与武断而非任何特定的经济制度造成的。

> "我用上了我所有的战斗本能，来捍卫我的异端观点：资本主义是造成分配不公、过度储蓄以及冒险帝国主义的经济动力的根源。这一度导致我过于简单地宣扬历史的经济决定论。"
>
> ——约翰·霍布森：《一个异端经济学家的自白》

整合

尽管霍布森的作品大多数都关注消费不足及帝国扩张主题，但是他的作品并不一定构成统一的整体。例如，霍布森最早期关于帝国主义的作品并不是反帝国主义的，而且在《帝国主义》出版后的创作生涯中，他并没有再坚持自己的结论。这一点在他1911年发表的《投资的经济学阐释》一文中可以看出。在该文中，他略微修正了先前的立场，认为许多投资企业联盟的国际化特征使金融家丧失"欲望或……能力"去敦促国家施行帝国主义政策。³

但是，一战之后，霍布森又一次对发达国家经济上的相互依赖能否取代军国主义（认为一个国家的目标可以通过军事行动得以实现）产生了悲观情绪。因此，他先是在1917年的著作《战后民主》中削弱了金融家的作用，而强调了政治家在推进外交军国主义方面的作用。接着，在1926年的著作《社会科学中的自由思想》中，他得出了这样的结论："帝国主义主要体现了人类的两种本能——武断与贪婪。"[4] 但是，《社会科学中的自由思想》一书也代表了霍布森研究范围的扩大，他开始思考社会科学的本质——以及人在社会中的本质——而不仅仅是某种特定的社会现象。

此时，霍布森更感兴趣的是如何将心理学融入政治经济学领域，他将人性视为帝国主义产生的一个独立原因，并且指出他最初的经济学解释只是不小心掩盖了该事实。从这个时候开始，他越来越关注总体的社会理论，而不是任何单一现象的理论。不过，霍布森的所有作品都呈现出一个共同特点：他非常关注政府如何通过干预，尤其是通过财富的再分配，来改善民众的生活。

意义

对霍布森作品的整体评价褒贬不一；除了"霍布森的少数好友、崇拜者以及志趣相投的社会批评家"之外，他在政治思想领域并没有产生广泛影响，直到多年后才引起关注。[5] 但是之后的思想家，包括俄国革命领袖弗拉基米尔·列宁和英国经济学家约翰·梅纳德·凯恩斯都将霍布森视为其灵感的直接来源。不过，霍布森的理论也并非完美，正如凯恩斯在1914年评价霍布森作品的全面影响时指出："每位读者在读到霍布森先生的新书时都会产生一种复杂的感情，既期待霍布森能从一个独立个体的立场对正统思想提出一些具有启发性且富有成效的批评，但也预料到其中会有不少诡辩、误解和有悖常理的思想。"[6]

这种整体评价说明，霍布森在《帝国主义》中的论点虽然极富洞见，但归根结底还是存在漏洞的。不过，正是因为其见解独到，《帝国主义》一书在世界范围内依旧发挥其影响，特别是在冷战期间，美国和苏联之间的国际权力争霸再次激发了人们对霍布森的关注。帝国主义批评家们重新提及霍布森，思考两个超级大国之间的国际冒险行为是否的确是受狭隘的经济利益所驱使。

不过，这些批评家并不一定都来自"霍布森学派"，因为他们并不认同霍布森的理论及其强烈主张，而是认同霍布森对发达国家采取国际军事计划所持的怀疑态度。

1. 约翰·霍布森：转引自 P. J. 凯恩《霍布森与帝国主义：激进主义、新自由主义与金融：1887—1938》，牛津：牛津大学出版社，2002年，第75页。
2. 约翰·霍布森：《一个异端经济学家的自白》，哈索克斯：哈维斯特出版社，1976年，第63页。
3. 约翰·霍布森：转引自迈克尔·斯奈德尔《J. A. 霍布森》，伦敦：麦克米伦出版社，1996年，第102页。
4. 斯奈德尔：《J. A. 霍布森》，第103页。
5. 迈克尔·弗雷登：《重估 J. A. 霍布森》，伦敦：恩温·海曼出版社，1990年，第3页。
6. 约翰·梅纳德·凯恩斯："《黄金、价格与薪酬》书评"，《经济期刊》，1913年第23期，第393页。

第三部分：学术影响

9 最初反响

要点

- 《帝国主义》刚出版时,不是受到批评,就是遭到冷遇,舆论普遍认为它没能证明金融家所实施的完美操纵这一"阴谋论"。
- 霍布森作出了回应,他试图将他的"阴谋论"与真实人物联系起来——因此夸大了塞西尔·罗兹*的地位。
- 《帝国主义》一书之所以出名,绝非因其理论,而是因为它提出了"帝国主义政策是非理性的"这一观点。当冷战重新引发了关于帝国主义政策的争论时,《帝国主义》一书便再次成为人们关注的话题。

批评

《帝国主义》一书在约翰·A.霍布森所属的激进主义者学术圈之外几乎没有产生直接影响。因此,霍布森最初遭遇的批评并非来自保守派或亲帝国主义者,而是来自他同行的自由派,他们认为霍布森夸大了事实。英国历史学教授P. J.凯恩写道:"即使是一些赞同霍布森观点的自由主义者和激进主义者也并没有过多关注《帝国主义》一书,因为他们认为该书'过于荒谬地夸大了'帝国主义的罪行。"[1]

以拉尔夫·莱恩为笔名的英国作家诺曼·安吉尔*是霍布森的主要批评家之一。他指出霍布森赋予了金融家阶层一种能够影响决策制定的近乎超人的能力,以及一种近乎不人道的冷淡态度。安吉尔写道:"这种弥漫全国的情绪如此之强烈——无论从哪个方面来说都是非理性的——以至于我们决不能认为这种情绪是由一小部分动机相当理性的团体所造成的或触发的。"[2]

对阴谋论的批评影响了霍布森论据的可信度，并且霍布森对全能金融家阶层这一刻板印象的定义不清也给他的理论造成了困扰。就连最支持《帝国主义》的报纸评论也并无恭维之词。《爱丁堡评论》认同安吉尔的观点，指出如果认为英国政策是由一群"金融家和百万富翁们的利己集团"在操纵的话，那就未免有点儿荒谬可笑，并且这些夸张的说法使得读者无法看到霍布森反对帝国主义政策这一观点的潜在力量与吸引力。³

> "霍布森笔下邪恶的资本家和他们的'寄生虫'只不过是一个假设，一种机械降神。这个假设只是为了在假定的人类理性与帝国政策的非理性之间寻找平衡：这本书就是呼吁回归一种理性的价值标准。那么他的错误在于认为这种平衡需要人为进行调整。"
> ——D.K.菲尔德豪斯："帝国主义：一种史学修正"，《经济史评论》

回应

虽然《帝国主义》于1905年得以再版，但是霍布森对文本只做了略微改动。英国历史学家P.J.凯恩列举了霍布森所做的几处改动："霍布森试图强化他关于外贸增长与现今帝国扩张之间的微弱联系的论述"，他重新将南非归为"热带"（即非白人）区域，从而和"白人聚集"（类似于澳大利亚和加拿大）区域形成区分。但是，他最终并未对核心观点进行大幅修改。⁴

1906年，即《帝国主义》再版后的一年，霍布森再版了他的第一部重要论著《现代资本主义的进化》，不过这并不是对他所受批评的一种直接回应。在该版《现代资本主义的进化》中，霍布森增加了一个新的章节，并采用一种比《帝国主义》更为具体的方式来阐释金融家阶层的主要权力。他主要关注英国企业巨头和政治家塞西尔·罗兹:"南非金融最显著的特征就是金融家们一直娴熟地利用政治机器来帮助他们提高和推销投资。那些构成工业开发与投机剥削物质基础的真实土地无不是他们通过非经济渠道、法律欺诈……和外交威胁等一系列手段获得的。"[5]

虽然霍布森指出了金融家们如何获得成功以及他们插手政治的倾向,但他依旧没有解决他对金融资本主义和帝国主义的区分中存在的漏洞。那么这个问题依然存在:金融家究竟如何行使如此巨大的权力,来影响政策的制定?

冲突与共识

围绕《帝国主义》的批判性争论在很大程度上是未果的,直到20世纪晚期才出现了一些富有建设性的学术讨论。此时,霍布森的阴谋论已经被抛弃,人们更倾向于认同国家与金融利益之间存在一套更为复杂的关系。

在霍布森20世纪所遭受的诸多批评之中,大英帝国研究专家、历史学家D. K. 菲尔德豪斯*对霍布斯的批评是最为彻底的。"霍布森观点的重要性和原创性仅仅在于他向英国及整个世界介绍了他对'帝国主义'一词所下的特殊定义。"[6]该定义认为帝国主义是为了满足帝国主义国家狭隘的资本主义利益而进行的一种堕落的剥削活动。菲尔德豪斯认为霍布森的帝国主义经济理论以及其对金融资本家的关注,更多的是"为时代撰写的一部小册子,而非对这一问题的严肃研究……其成功之处在于它用一种极其清晰、有力和坚定的方式表达了一种现行观点。"[7]

菲尔德豪斯最终发现霍布森的经济理论是不完善的,因为它没能恰当地解释资本输出:"通过仔细研究可以发现,虽然欧洲投资者据说有……为他们的过剩资本寻找出口的需求,但这与欧洲列强瓜分非洲及太平洋地区的行径几乎或者根本没有关系。"而且,1870年后的帝国扩张主要源自于保护现有财产的需求,并且"从经济角度来看",这种动机很大程度上并没有改变。[8]

不过,虽然菲尔德豪斯已经指出了这些问题,但他仍然认为霍布森的分析有一个主要价值,即它宣称帝国主义整体上是非理性的。但是由于霍布森不能从字面上接受这一说法,他不得不编造一个金融家的阴谋,对金融家来说,帝国主义具有其合理性——菲尔德豪斯认为这些人物都只不过是"一个假设……为了在假定的人类理性与帝国政策的非理性之间取得平衡。"[9]

---

1. P. J. 凯恩:《霍布森与帝国主义:激进主义、新自由主义与金融:1887—1938》,牛津:牛津大学出版社,2002年,第163—164页。
2. 诺曼·安吉尔:转引自凯恩,《霍布森与帝国主义》,第118—119页。
3. 提莫·萨卡:《霍布森的帝国主义:维多利亚晚期政治思想研究》,韦斯屈莱:韦斯屈莱大学出版社,2009年,第166页。
4. 凯恩:《霍布森与帝国主义》,第171—172页。
5. 约翰·霍布森:《现代资本主义的进化》,伦敦:沃尔特·司各特出版公司,1906年,第266页。
6. D. K. 菲尔德豪斯:"帝国主义:一种史学修正",《经济史评论》第14卷,1961年第2期,第187页。
7. 菲尔德豪斯:"帝国主义",第189页。
8. 菲尔德豪斯:"帝国主义",第213页。
9. 菲尔德豪斯:"帝国主义",第214页。

10 后续争议

要点

- 霍布森的《帝国主义》最先发起了关于国内经济利益与国外政治侵略之间关系的争辩,而对贸易与种族伦理的争辩则未加关注。
- 弗拉基米尔·列宁和波兰裔德籍革命活动家罗莎·卢森堡*等马克思主义思想家借用并发展了霍布森的观点,以号召民众进行革命而非社会改革;现代马克思主义思想家艾伦·梅克辛斯·伍德*和大卫·哈维*致力于研究非正式、"隐蔽的"帝国主义形式。
- 美国政治理论家迈克尔·哈特和意大利哲学家安东尼奥·内格里等后马克思主义*者(拒绝接受马克思主义理论的某些核心原则的思想家)认为,21世纪的帝国并非受一种力量控制,而是资本主义操纵一切的"一种状态"。

应用与问题

霍布森的核心概念——军国主义、资本主义和帝国主义的关系——于20世纪早期在研究帝国主义权力的学者那里得到了发展。

被霍布森对资本帝国主义的批判所吸引的最著名的马克思主义理论家是弗拉基米尔·列宁,他是苏联第一位共产主义*总理。列宁回应霍布森的观点并写道:"帝国主义是资本主义的垄断阶段……在该阶段资本的输出已经变得尤为重要。"[1] 两位思想家的主要区别在于对帝国主义开出了不同的药方:霍布森认为该危机可通过再分配得以解决,而列宁却认为摆脱帝国主义的唯一方法就是彻底摆脱资本主义。

虽然奥地利经济学家与政治思想家约瑟夫·熊彼特*赞同帝国主义中包含经济与军事因素这一观点，但他还是推翻了霍布森的论点。霍布森认为经济因素反过来滋生了军国主义，而熊彼特却从理论上证明帝国主义根植于军国主义，在这之后经济原因才能成立。"（国家战争机器）是由必要的战争所创造，现在它又以经济原因为借口创造了它所需要的战争。"² 但是，熊彼特和霍布森都认同军国主义会带来非自由主义*后果（即损害个人自由的后果）。

德国政治思想家汉娜·阿伦特*又进一步发展了这种观点，并在其重要论著《极权主义的起源》中重申了她的伦理立场。她在书中写道，帝国主义源于资本主义思想（特别是追求无限制的发展）在公共领域的传播；"帝国主义的核心思想是将扩张作为永恒而至高的政治目标。"³ 对于阿伦特来说，永恒扩张的意识形态打破了政治的伦理与道德界限——这与霍布森对国外帝国主义政策会破坏国内自由政治的担忧相呼应。

> "需要强调的是，我们这里使用的'帝国'一词并不是取其隐喻意义……而是作为一种概念，该概念首先需要一种理论方法来支撑。帝国概念最根本的特征就是缺乏疆界：帝国的统治没有界限。那么，首先也是最重要的就是帝国概念假设有这样一个政体，它可以有效地涵盖所有空间或实际上统治整个'文明'世界。它的统治没有任何领域限制。"
> ——迈克尔·哈特和安东尼奥·内格里：《帝国》

思想流派

霍布森在《帝国主义》中使用的科学论证方法历来吸引了众多

马克思主义者。不过，尽管他们整体都认同资本过剩与帝国主义有关，但他们对导致这种整体状况的原因及解决方法有不同的看法。马克思主义者们都持一种决定论观点，认为资本主义是历史的必然阶段，而帝国主义是资本主义发展的最高阶段。因此，通过暴力推翻资本主义和寻找帝国主义的解决办法实际上是一回事——这与霍布森主张建立的一种更友好、平等的资本主义形成了鲜明对比。

波兰裔德籍马克思主义思想家罗莎·卢森堡认为，"殖民（发展中）国家需要从资本主义国家获取资金以求发展，从而为那些资本主义国家开辟市场。"[4] 基于该观点，她提出了自己的帝国主义理论。换句话说，资本主义需要不断开拓新的市场来维持盈利，也就是说，资本主义国家之间将会就非资本主义国家展开争夺——"但是，帝国主义越是通过暴力、残酷和彻底的方法来引发非资本主义文明的没落，它就会越快地切断资本主义积累赖以存在的根基。"[5] 换句话说，帝国主义不仅仅是在输出资本，而且也在创造更多的资本主义社会。

20世纪后期的马克思主义思想家，特别是英国社会地理学家戴维·哈利和加拿大历史学家艾伦·梅克辛斯·伍德，对国家在帝国主义政策制定过程中所扮演的角色提出了质疑。他们认为，虽然现代帝国主义在很大程度上呈现出非地域性和非扩张性特征，但它主要依赖于国家霸权*（或支配地位）和军事行动的不断威胁。[6] 权力定义了"（高度发达国家与欠发达国家之间）交换关系的不对称性，通过施加体制性压力迫使全世界开放市场……这种体制性压力往往是通过（诸如国际货币基金组织*和世界银行*这样的）金融机构来施加，而这些金融机构又都靠美国在背后撑腰……这样他国就无法进入美国自己庞大的市场。"[7]

当代研究

对帝国进行批判的最著名的两位后马克思主义批评家是迈克尔·哈特和安东尼奥·内格里。两者都认为"帝国"是资本主义所定义的一种全球化体制，不过它并不以任何一个国家为中心。资本主义制度使一些国家具有凌驾于其他国家之上的利益与特权（比如，和发展中国家相比，美国拥有更多利益与特权），同时也形成了诸如国际货币基金组织和世界银行等国际组织、跨国公司以及强势国家之间社会关系的网络。

霍布森认为，资本向民族国家发号施令；而在哈特和内格里看来，资本已经取代了民族国家。他们写道："帝国概念的基本特征是缺乏疆界：帝国统治没有界限。"[8] 首先，他们认为这意味着帝国包含了整个世界；其次，帝国并不是任何一个国家操控的，相反，它是"一种状态"；最后，"帝国的运转涵盖了社会秩序的所有方面，一直延伸到社会世界的深处。"[9] 在他们的范式或模型中，全球化*（世界范围的）资本主义的权力并不是由一些掌握权力的个体以牺牲他人利益为代价而操控的，而是这种权力本身已经非常强大，以至于它控制了整个世界的人口，包括"剥削者"与"被剥削者"，决定了他们是谁以及他们之间的关系。

从本质上讲，哈特和内格里已经脱离了霍布森的一些核心思想，比如资本家和政治家压迫帝国属地臣民的这种单向关系，而是强调资本主义日益增长的力量。在霍布森看来，资本主义决定国家政策；在哈特和内格里看来，资本主义的上升势头已经形成，它已无处不在并开始定义一切。

1. 弗拉基米尔·列宁:《帝国主义是资本主义的最高阶段》, 纽约: 国际出版社, 1939年, 第88—89页。
2. 约瑟夫·熊彼特:《帝国主义与社会阶层: 两篇文章》, 海因茨·诺登译, 纽约: 莫瑞迪安出版社, 2007年, 第25页。
3. 汉娜·阿伦特:《极权主义的起源》, 纽约: 哈考特出版社, 1968年, 第125页。
4. 菲利普·阿雷斯蒂斯和马尔科姆·索亚:《埃尔加激进政治经济学导读》, 奥尔德肖特: 爱德华·埃尔加出版社, 1994年, 第21页。
5. 罗莎·卢森堡:《资本的积累》, 登录日期2014年2月22日, http://www.marxists.org/archive/luxemburg/1913/accumulation-capital/ch31.htm。
6. 艾伦·梅克辛斯·伍德:《资本的帝国》, 伦敦: 福尔索出版社, 2005年, 第130页。
7. 大卫·哈维:《新帝国主义》, 牛津: 牛津大学出版社, 2005年, 第32页。
8. 迈克尔·哈特和安东尼奥·内格里:《帝国》, 马萨诸塞州坎布里奇: 哈佛大学出版社, 2000年, 第XV页。
9. 哈特和内格里:《帝国》, 第XV页。

11 当代印迹

要点

- 在当今的学术辩论中,霍布森已不再是一个"积极"的参与者——他的重要性在于他洞察到私人利益缘何能够颠覆一个国家。
- 根据新现实主义*流派的国际关系(即国家之间的相互作用)理论,所有国家的对外侵略行为都来自理性的权力算计;社会理论学家大卫·哈维和艾伦·梅克辛斯·伍德作出回应,指出伊拉克战争*在政治上是非理性的,但在经济上却是合理的。
- 根据新现实主义的国际关系理论,任何国家都不会冒险通过战争来追寻经济利益,因为风险太大了;美国在海外作战是为了按照自己的构想来重塑世界并确保其安全。

地位

约翰·霍布森1902年的著作《帝国主义》不再是当前经济与政治论辩的关注焦点。总的来说,霍布森之所以受到称赞,与其说是由于其理论本身,不如说是因为他最早发起了对帝国主义的批判,并将其视为一种符合少数人利益的经济现象而非政治现象。

美国经济学家格雷戈里·诺埃尔*对待霍布森的态度可以作为一个例子:"我们现在还在谈论霍布森吗?是的,也不是。霍布森的核心论点是寡头政治*(由少数人统治的政府)和寡头垄断*(少数生产商对市场的控制),以及它们对政治制度、社会对投资的控制能力和收入再分配的影响。"诺埃尔写道,"这才是真正的霍布森,正是他吸引了现代读者,而不只是那个被狭隘理解的阐释殖民

主义的学者。"¹

虽然霍布森关于英帝国主义的分析对历史和思想史的研究非常重要，但是从政治学与经济学角度来看却分量不重——这限制了他对资本主义权力的分析。² 现代马克思主义代表人物如大卫·哈维和艾伦·梅克辛斯·伍德拒绝接受霍布森的"阴谋论"，而支持一种更为普遍的假设，即美国企业与政府的利益是大体一致的。³ 哈维和梅克辛斯·伍德在分析军事行动与资本主义扩张的关系时都受到过霍布森的启发。"对全球经济的无限控制，"梅克辛斯·伍德写道，"以及对管理全球经济的诸多国家的控制，无论在目的还是时间上都需要持续不断地采取军事行动。"⁴ 同理，两者都认为帝国主义与"全球霸权"（也就是一种占据主导地位的力量）的需求有关；帝国主义要么是由资本主义强国发起的（哈维），要么是由大体上支持资本主义的国家集团所发起的（梅克辛斯·伍德）。

> "霍布森《帝国主义》的主要论点在过去和现在都有助于理解资本主义。"
>
> ——格雷戈里·诺埃尔："霍布森的《帝国主义》"，《帝国主义的政治经济学》

互动

美国政治理论家肯尼斯·华尔兹*在著作《国际政治理论》（1979）中从新现实主义学派的角度对霍布森的论点进行了批判性分析。

新现实主义认为国家行为可以从相对权力的角度来理解；也就是说，一个国家总是想超越他国并使其权力最大化，强权国家以寻求区域霸权（主导地位）为终极目标。⁵ 这些理论家认为美国在后冷战时代对全球政治的主导地位可作为一个例证。

换句话说，由肯尼斯·华尔兹提出并由政治理论家约翰·米尔斯海默*在其著作《大国政治的悲剧》（2001）中进一步发展的新现实主义思想，对霍布森的分析构成了一种具有说服力的挑战。

但是，许多从事帝国主义权力研究的现代理论家纷纷对"外国冲突是受国家安全利益所驱使的"这一新现实主义观点作出了回应。比如大卫·哈维会对新现实主义的立场提出反对，认为新现实主义理论家将入侵伊拉克的行为视为非理性的观点是错误的，而他认为从狭隘的经济视角来看，入侵是理性的。

哈维写道，"当约瑟夫·张伯伦*在20世纪初带领英国卷入布尔战争时，很明显，英国的首要动机是黄金与钻石储备。"反过来，这使得英国国内过度积累的资本能够在国外得到投资。[6]同样地，他认为："（乔治·W.布什总统*）执政期间对中东地区进行武力干涉的动机就是为了获得对中东地区原油资源更加强硬的控制……（并且）原油价格的整体下跌可以被视为一种策略，旨在应对过去30年间出现的资本过度积累这一长期问题。"[7]

就像霍布森论及的布尔战争一样，哈维认为伊拉克战争从金融资本主义的角度来看是理性的，但是从公共利益与战略利益的角度来看却是非理性的。[8]

梅克辛斯·伍德声称美国的"经济帝国将通过复杂国家体系下的政治和军事霸权来维持"，而且这个经济帝国尤其关注如何打开一个"能够为西方资本提供输出的第三世界"。[9]她同时列举了自己与哈维对于资本帝国主义观点的差异："他提出资本积累的持续扩张必然伴随着政治权力的持续扩大和对领土的控制，而这就是资本帝国主义的逻辑。我却持相反观点：资本帝国主义的特殊性在于资本具有一种不必通过扩张领土政治权就能施加霸权的独特能力……资本主义本身就创造了一种自主的经济统制形式。"[10]

持续争议

新现实主义流派从一开始就对霍布森和当代马克思主义者提出了质疑；实际上，肯尼斯·华尔兹将《帝国主义》视为一种错误理论的例证。华尔兹认为，许多不同类型的国家，包括一些非资本主义国家，都已经采取了帝国主义政策。他写道，"对（霍布斯）理论的接受"是基于"它从经济视角进行论证这一方法的吸引力以及现今发达的资本主义国家确实是历史上最令人印象深刻的帝国缔造者这个赤裸裸的事实……那么为什么不将资本主义和帝国主义等同起来呢？"[11] 华尔兹这样回答自己的问题："各种类型的国家，"包括非资本主义的苏联，"都奉行帝国主义的政策。"[12] 因此，经济视角的阐释不能充分解释这个宏大战略背后的原因。

米尔斯海默在某种程度上认同美国正在采取一种帝国主义的外交政策，并且这种外交政策由于鼓励军国主义和一种"安全文化"而威胁到国内自由。[13] 米尔斯海默和霍布森也赞同"国内因素引发帝国主义计划"的观点。[14] 但是，他们对帝国主义计划背后的原因存在分歧。米尔斯海默写道，"美国问题的根源就在于它在冷战后采取了一种错误的宏大战略……寻求全球统治地位，或者可称为是一种全球霸权。"[15]

但是如果这种计划不是以经济利益为目标，那么它又是以什么为目标呢？对于米尔斯海默来说，答案是显而易见的："确保美国仍然是国际体系中最强大的国家；同时，在全球范围内推行民主，不过这实际上是以美国的形象来塑造世界。"[16] 从本质上讲，现代新现实主义认为美国追求权力时首先思考的是安全，而经济动机则无关紧要。因此，虽然一些现代帝国主义的批评家（如哈维与梅克辛斯·伍德）认为2003年美国入侵伊拉克是对资本主义利益的理性追求，但华尔兹与米尔斯海默却认为这不过是美国所犯下的一个极大的错误。

---

1. 格雷戈里·诺埃尔："霍布森的《帝国主义》：历史有效性与当代关联性"，载《帝国主义的政治经济学：批判性评估》，马里兰州拉纳姆：罗曼和利特菲尔德出版社，1999年，第102页。
2. 诺埃尔："霍布森的《帝国主义》"，第104页。
3. 大卫·哈维：《新帝国主义》，牛津：牛津大学出版社，2005年，第18页。
4. 艾伦·梅克辛斯·伍德：《资本帝国》，伦敦：华尔索出版社，2005年，第144页。
5. 约翰·米尔斯海默：《大国政治的悲剧》，纽约：W. W. 诺顿出版社，2001年，第169页。
6. 哈维：《新帝国主义》，第180页。
7. 哈维：《新帝国主义》，第180页。
8. 约翰·霍布森：《帝国主义》，诺丁汉：斯伯克斯曼出版社，2011年，第85页。
9. 梅克辛斯·伍德：《资本帝国》，第130页。
10. 艾伦·梅克辛斯·伍德："权力的逻辑：大卫·哈维访谈"，《历史唯物主义》第14卷，2006年第4期，第13页。
11. 肯尼斯·华尔兹：《国际政治理论》，马里兰州雷丁：艾迪逊·韦斯雷出版社，1979年，第25页。
12. 华尔兹：《国际政治理论》，第36页。
13. 约翰·米尔斯海默："帝国主义设计"，《国家利益》，2011年第111期，第17页。
14. 霍布森：《帝国主义》，第142页。
15. 米尔斯海默："帝国主义设计"，第18页。
16. 米尔斯海默："帝国主义设计"，第19页。

12 未来展望

要点 ⚷

- 只要各国仍推行与经济利益挂钩的侵略性外交政策，那么霍布森的作品就依旧具有现实意义。
- 《帝国主义》延续了对资本主义进行批判的长期传统，认为资本主义制度受到"操纵"而导致阶层不平等——法国经济学家托马斯·皮凯蒂*的著作《21世纪资本论》可被视作该传统的延续。
- 《帝国主义》的重要性不在于它提出的核心论点，而在于它揭示了驱动资本主义扩张的关系网——尽管现在人们对这些关系网还知之甚少。

潜力

加拿大学者迈克尔·伊格纳季耶夫*坚持认为美国的"反恐战争"*是对其帝国主义侵略行为的一种修辞性的掩饰：他认为尽管美国没有公然吞并海外领土，但美国的外交政策依然具有帝国主义特性。"看看美国遍布全球的军队、间谍和特种部队，这难道不是一种帝国主义势力吗？"[1]你可以称之为一种诡计。这种后霍布森视角将"反恐战争"视为美国为其外国干预进行辩护的手段，而不是美国安全利益的真实体现。

除此之外，霍布森的帝国主义概念要求帝国主义计划应确保私人经济利益——而这往往要以公众利益为代价。美国前总统德怀特·D.艾森豪威尔*在其《告别演说》中揭示了军国主义与帝国扩张之间的关系以及公众为之承受的代价。实际上，令人印象深刻的是他创造了"军工综合体"*这个术语,并发出警示:"在政府委员会中,我们必须警惕由军工综合体有意或无意间施加的一些干预所带来的后果。"2

根据艾森豪威尔的观点,允许不同的利益群体来共同控制政策制定将会降低国内的自由度,并强化国外的军国主义行为。对该综合体的焦虑一直持续至今,这在2014年《独立报》上发表的一篇文章《艾克一直都是对的》中可窥见一斑。在该文中,英国记者鲁伯特·康维尔*写道:"真正的悲剧并不完全是艾森豪威尔所想象的那样。美国自身的军费支出约占全球军费支出的一半。如果这些钱中的一部分能够用来提高国家的教育和基础设施建设,或者为全民提供医保,或者增加对外援助,而不是保护美国免受各种假想的威胁(地理决定了这些威胁不可能存在),那样该有多好啊!"3

霍布森断言,国外的军国主义行为将会最终破坏国内的自由,而这一观点已进入公众话语。美国法律专家杰弗里·罗森*对《美国爱国者法案》(USA PATRIOT Act)*的批判就是一个例子。缩略语PATRIOT的全称是"为拦截和阻止恐怖主义提供合适的手段",它明显唤起了美国民众的爱国主义情绪,但也掩盖了该法案背后的真实行为与危险性:"从一开始,对《爱国者法案》提出批判的民主党和共和党人就警告称,如此强大的监控手段会被用来调查一些政治异端分子或低级别犯罪,而不是用来对抗恐怖主义……司法部监察长在2007年发布的报告中指出,联邦调查局*在《爱国者法案》的指导下,存在广泛而严重的滥用权力行为——即使这些行为与恐怖主义并没有明显关系。"4

> "这种将庞大的军事机构和庞大的军火工业进行联合的做法在美国历史上还从未有过。所有这一切影响——无论是经济的、政治的还是精神的——在每个城市、每个州议会以及联邦政府的每个办公室都能被感受到。"
>
> —— 德怀特·D. 艾森豪威尔:《告别演说》

未来方向

霍布森所发起的关于帝国主义的讨论中,最令人兴奋并有持续影响的内容与经济学有关。

法国经济学家托马斯·皮凯蒂在《21 世纪资本论》(2014)一书中提出了这样一个假设:"我们根本没有理由去相信任何发展都会自动走向平衡",并且资本主义发展带来了更多而非更少的不平等。[5] 皮凯蒂的首个主要结论是财富的分配并非"经济决定论"的后果——资本主义经济体制并没有一套内在的法则来确保财富的平均分配。[6]

最重要的是——为了从霍布森的观点中得出一个自然结论——皮凯蒂认为"财富分配的历史一直以来都是具有浓厚政治色彩的"。[7] 因此,皮凯蒂与霍布森的理论在"富人阶层如何被赋予与其地位不匹配的政治权力"方面存在共同之处。在霍布森看来,这就是富人阶层如何教唆政治家推行帝国主义政策从而确保他们在海外的资本投资;在皮凯蒂看来,这就是关于财富分配的政治决策如何确保富人阶层的利益。

皮凯蒂的专著还提出了另一个核心论点:那些大公司的高层能够并且经常为了自己的利益而串通起来采取行动,却往往背离公众利益——这与霍布森的阴谋论有很多相似之处,但是两者之间存在两点重要区别。

首先，皮凯蒂认为这种勾结通常发生在商界内部而非商界与政府之间（正如霍布森认为的那样）。其次，皮凯蒂对于该观点的推理非常清晰，不会轻易走向概念性滑移（就像霍布森那样）。但是两者均提出这种勾结的本质是极其简单的："整体而言，顶层管理者往往有权力决定如何分配自身酬金。"换句话说，他们商定自己的薪水——并且他们恰巧将那个数字定得非常高。[8]

实际上，根据美国劳工联合会—产业工会联合会这一美国工会组织于 2014 年发布的一项报告，美国首席执行官的工资是公司员工工资的 331 倍——而在 1983 年，这一数字接近 50 倍。[9]

小结

约翰·霍布森《帝国主义》（1902）值得我们特别关注，因为它仍然是英国政治激进主义传统中对帝国主义政策最有力、最尖锐的批评之一。

这部著作一方面启发弗拉基米尔·列宁创作了《帝国主义是资本主义的最高阶段》一书，并且从 20 世纪至今，马克思主义思想一直深受其启发。历史学家 D. K. 菲尔德豪斯作为 20 世纪对《帝国主义》批评最激烈的学者之一，也列举了《帝国主义》的一系列成就：霍布森证明了帝国主义是一种非理性的公共政策，他促使"英国及世界接受他对帝国主义一词所下的特殊定义。"[10]

霍布森对帝国主义的"特殊"定义不仅指一种向国界之外推进的军事冒险行动：它更多地指以开拓市场、开发资源、输出资本为目的的资本主义计划。霍布森认为，所有这些都不过是一个盘算已久的计划，该计划通过蛊惑公众意识来确保私人投资者的主要收益，而这一切都是以宗主国和殖民地的公共利益为代价的。

由于霍布森将金融家描绘成凌驾于国家之上的无所不能的权力掮客，因此他的分析通常被视为一种阴谋论而不太被关注。不过尽管如此，霍布森的理论仍有足够的力量成为一种必需的基本观点。其实，今天变得无所不能的正是资本主义本身，因此对于今天的读者与思想家而言，《帝国主义》一书仍然具有价值。

---

1. 迈克尔·伊格纳季耶夫："轻国家构建"，《纽约时报》，2002年7月28日，登录日期2014年2月22日，http://www.nytimes.com/2002/07/28magazine/nation-building-lite.html。
2. 德怀特·D.艾森豪威尔：《告别演说》，登录日期2014年2月17日，http://www.americanrhetoric.com/speeches/dwightdeisenhowerfarewell.html。
3. 鲁伯特·康维尔："艾克一直都是对的：军工综合体的危险"，2011年1月17日，登录日期2014年2月22日，http://www.independent.co.uk/news/world/americas/ike-was-right-all-along-the-danger-of-the-militaryindustrial-complex-2186133.html。
4. 杰弗里·罗森："过多权力？"《国际纽约时报》，2007年9月7日，登录日期2014年2月22日，http://www.nytimes.com/roomfordebate/2011/09/07/do-we-still-need-the-patriot-act/the-patriot-act-gives-too-much-power-to-law-enforcement。
5. 托马斯·皮凯蒂、安东尼·阿特肯逊和伊曼纽尔·赛斯：《21世纪资本论》，马塞诸塞州坎布里奇：贝尔纳普出版社，2014年，第15页。
6. 皮凯蒂等：《21世纪资本论》，第20页。
7. 皮凯蒂等：《21世纪资本论》，第20页。
8. 皮凯蒂等：《21世纪资本论》，第24页。
9. "派沃切公司2014年度报告"，美国劳工联合会——产业工会联合会报告，登录日期2015年7月9日，http://edit.aflcio.org/Corporate-Watch/Paywatch-2014。
10. D.K.菲尔德豪斯："帝国主义：一种史学修正"，《经济历史批评》第14卷，1961年第2期，第187页。

术语表

1. 反犹太主义：对犹太人的歧视或仇恨。

2. 布尔战争（1899—1902）：大英帝国与布尔共和国（位于现在的南非，当时被荷兰移民后裔布尔人所占领统治）之间爆发的冲突。战争结束后，大英帝国吞并了布尔领土，双方都付出了巨大的军事与民事代价。

3. 资本主义：生产资料（主要是资源与工厂）归个人所有的一种经济制度，以在市场经济中出售商品赚取利润为目的。

4. 古典自由主义：该政治思想主张限制国家权力以确保最大程度的个人自由，主张财产私有制与最低限度的干预。

5. 冷战（1947—1991）：美国与苏联及同盟国之间的紧张对峙时期。虽然两大阵营从未发生过正面军事冲突，但却暗地发起较为隐蔽的代理人战争（在军事冲突中赞助对方的反对派）以及相互开展间谍活动。

6. 殖民主义：根据霍布森的理解，殖民主义指的是发达国家向未经开发的地区进行人口迁移，并向移民赋予全部公民权利。霍布森将殖民主义视为帝国主义的对立面。

7. 共产主义：主张生产资料国有化、劳动集体化以及废除社会阶级的一种政治意识形态。共产主义曾是苏联（1922—1991）时期的社会意识形态，与冷战期间的自由市场资本主义形成对比。

8. 集中营：一种类似监狱的设施，关押的是被国家视为敌人的非军事人员。集中营的生活条件极其恶劣，且往往不经过法庭判决而直接拘留。

9. 欧洲中心主义：该观点认为欧洲文化史提供了某种"标准"，并以此标准评判所有其他文化。

10. 费边社：1884年成立的一个英国社会主义组织，其目的是通过长期施压来影响议会进程。

11. **联邦调查局（FBI）**：美国专门负责调查间谍活动、恐怖主义及重大犯罪行为的政府机构。

12. **金融资本主义**：资本主义经济中专门与金融（以私人利润为目的的私人投资）有关的部分。

13. **金融家**：对企业进行投资、收购或提供巨额贷款的职业人士。

14. **全球化**：由思想、文化与物质商品在全球范围内的交流与交换而引起的一系列国际一体化过程（可以是有计划的也可以是自发的）。

15. **霸权**：一个国家或军事团体以各种形式凌驾于他国之上。

16. **非自由主义的**：与自由主义的政治信条相反，要么对促进个人自由漠不关心，要么积极限制个人自由。

17. **帝国主义**：霍布森认为帝国主义是一国以经济利益为目的而夺取他国领土的行为。

18. **制度经济学**：研究现有制度与观念在塑造经济行为方面的作用。

19. **国际货币基金组织（IMF）**：以促进合作、确保良好金融治理为宗旨的国际机构。

20. **伊拉克战争（2003—2011）**：最初是发生在伊拉克和美国及其同盟国之间的一场武装冲突；当美国与其同盟国实现最初的军事目标后，一场旷日持久的叛乱就开始了。美国以伊拉克领导人萨达姆·侯赛因私造大规模杀伤性武器为由发起了战争，但是最终并没有找到所谓的大规模杀伤性武器。

21. **沙文主义**：一种极端的爱国主义。

22. **列宁帝国主义**：俄国革命领袖弗拉基米尔·列宁提出的一套帝国主义理论，该理论与霍布森的观点有诸多相似之处。列宁认为中产阶级金融家将资本输出到发展中国家，从而剥削穷人。他和霍布森观点的不同之处在于他认为这种剥削是为了防止国内下层阶级进行革命，而革命是根除资本主义与帝国主义的唯一途径。

23. **自由党**（1859—1988）：英国的一个政治党派。该党派支持福利制度，积极推进贸易。1988年，自由党与社会民主党合并，形成了现今依然活跃的自由民主党。

24. **自由主义**：一种支持个人自由与福利制度的政治思想。

25. **马克思主义**：一种包罗万象的以唯物主义、阶级斗争和决定论为主要内容的社会分析学派，以德国政治哲学家卡尔·马克思的著作为理论依据。

26. **重商主义**：19世纪以前西欧国家的主导经济政策。重商主义旨在促进贸易的良性平衡（认为贸易应以国内贸易为主），因此是殖民扩张的核心驱动力。

27. **军国主义**：主张军队是国家最重要的组成部分并且使用武力是外交政策中较为适当的（通常也是必要的）一个因素。

28. **军工综合体**：美国立法者、军事将领及私人军火工业之间的关系网络。

29. **民族主义**：一种极端的爱国主义，通常伴有对他国的蔑视。

30. **新现实主义**：国际关系理论的一个流派，认为结构性限制——无政府状态和世界权力的分布——将会决定行动者的行为，而不是人的能动性。

31. **新自由主义**：主张通过政府干预来确保经济与社会公平的一种自由主义思想。

32. **寡头政治**：由少数人操纵一切的政治局面。

33. **寡头垄断**：少数生产商主导市场的一种状态。

34. **爱国者法案**（2001）：美国的一条立法，该立法赋予美国执法机构前所未有的权力来对美国公民实施监控。也称作《美国爱国者法案》。

35. **爱国主义**：对自己国家的热爱与崇拜。

36. **政治经济学**：经济学的一个学术领域分支。"政治经济学"通常研究政治体制与机构如何影响国家经济运行。

37. **后马克思主义**：在批判传统马克思主义核心观点的基础上重新建构的思想学派。比如，后马克思主义者不赞同马克思提出的"资本家把国家当作工具"的观点；对他们而言，"国家"这一概念在本质上具有"资本主义特征"。

38. **累进税制**：指随着应纳税额的增加而逐级提高税率的一种制度；由此产生的平均税率低于最高边际税率。

39. **原型**：某些产品或服务的"第一批蓝本"（通常作为一种"概念试验品"）。

40. **激进主义**（18—19世纪）：主张通过改革选举制度来扩大选举权范围的英国左翼政治运动。该运动后来也泛指为了强化政治自由主义的各种思想运动。

41. **萨伊定律**：以法国经济学家让-巴蒂斯特·萨伊（1767—1832）的名字命名的理论。萨伊定律认为生产是需求的来源。换句话说，当个体生产产品时，他将会得到报酬，然后去购买他人生产的产品，他人反过来又会购买他的产品，依此类推。

42. **非洲争夺战**（1881—1914）：指欧洲列强在非洲领土上大肆扩张，宣布对殖民地的直接统治权并掠夺其资源的历史时期。

43. **社会达尔文主义**：运用科学语言和（所谓的）科学方法来解释种族主义观点。20世纪30年代至40年代，德国纳粹党主要推行社会达尔文主义，作为其种族主义/反犹太主义政治纲领的一部分。该术语现今含有贬义色彩。

44. **社会自由主义**：主张自由（自由主义）应当通过国家机构（社会主义）得到保障的政治观点。社会自由主义者主张市场经济及再分配计划。

45. **社会主义**：主张商品生产要素应归"社会"（人民）所有而非个人资本家所有的一种政治信仰。

46. **苏联**：1922年至1991年间俄罗斯及其东欧与亚洲北半部邻国形成的共产主义国家联盟。冷战期间，苏联代表了共产主义阵营，与美国代表的资本主义阵营形成"对抗"。

47. **工会**：同行业内形成的劳工组织，旨在与劳动力购买商进行协商并影响政策制定。

48. **消费不足理论**：该理论认为当供给大于需求时会导致经济停滞。20世纪30年代，该理论在很大程度上被凯恩斯的总需求理论所取代，后者是从经济学家约翰·梅纳德·凯恩斯的观点中衍生而来的理论。

49. **"反恐战争"**：指美国在中东地区发起的针对非国家"恐怖主义"组织，包括"基地"组织和"伊斯兰国"。巴基斯坦的无人机行动、占领阿富汗的行动以及其他一些公开或隐蔽的行动都与此相关。

50. **世界银行**：以管理经济援助、向成员国提供贷款以使其克服金融危机为宗旨的国际金融机构。

51. **第一次世界大战**：也称"世界大战"，发生在1914年至1918年间。在战争期间，协约国（以法国、意大利、俄罗斯、英国和美国为首）与同盟国（以奥地利—匈牙利、保加利亚、德国和奥斯曼帝国为首）作战，导致1 600万人丧命。

人名表

1. 诺曼·安吉尔（1872—1967），英国讲师、作家，唯心主义学派国际关系研究的重要代表人物。

2. 汉娜·阿伦特（1906—1975），德国政治思想家。她的作品主要探讨权力与控制的本质。

3. 迈克尔·巴拉特·布朗（1918—2015），英国政治经济学家、马克思主义学者，对外交政策尤其感兴趣。

4. 杰里米·边沁（1748—1832），英国哲学家、自由主义社会改革家，被视为功利主义哲学的创始人（功利主义哲学认为人的行为应以它是否能给人带来快乐来判断其好坏）。

5. 乔治·W. 布什（1946年生），美国政治家，于2001年至2009年间担任美国第43任总统。布什在任期间，美国在2001年遭遇了9·11恐怖袭击事件，随后于2003年入侵伊拉克，并对阿富汗进行持续占领。

6. P. J. 凯恩（1941年生），英国谢菲尔德大学历史学教授，主要研究英国自由思想史。

7. 约瑟夫·张伯伦（1836—1914），英国政治家，曾指挥第二次布尔战争并担任殖民地国务大臣。

8. 理查德·科布登（1804—1865），英国商人与自由主义政治家，主张一种自由主义的国际政治观。

9. 杰里米·科尔宾（1949年生），英国国会议员，2015年9月起担任英国工党领袖。

10. 鲁伯特·康维尔，英国记者，主要担任伦敦《独立报》的驻美通讯记者。

11. 德怀特·D. 艾森豪威尔（1890—1969），美国政治家、将军，曾任美

国总统（1953—1961）。

12. 戴维·肯尼斯·菲尔德豪斯（1925年生），剑桥大学耶稣学院从事大英帝国研究的历史学家。

13. 托马斯·希尔·格林（1836—1882），英国自由主义哲学家，以提出消极自由（不受限制的自由）与积极自由（被赋予某种能力的自由）的区分而著称。

14. 迈克尔·哈特（1960年生），美国文学理论家与政治哲学家。

15. 大卫·哈维（1935年生），英国地理学教授，执教于纽约城市大学，主要研究社会理论，被誉为马克思主义全球资本主义批评的首要核心人物之一。

16. 迈克尔·伊格纳季耶夫（1947年生），加拿大学者，从事国际发展研究，曾是一名自由主义政治家。

17. 约翰·梅纳德·凯恩斯男爵（1883—1946），英国经济学家，被誉为现代宏观经济学的创始人，因为他证明了完全自由市场并不能提供充分就业。

18. 弗拉基米尔·列宁（1870—1924），俄国共产主义革命政治家，是苏联首位总理。

19. 约翰·洛克（1632—1704），英国哲学家，古典自由主义学派的创始人之一，主张强调个人自由，限制政府权力。他是社会契约学派的主要思想家。他的作品《政府论·下篇》被公认为一部开拓性著作。

20. 戴维·朗，加拿大卡尔顿大学国际关系教授。

21. 约翰·朗斯代尔，剑桥大学三一学院的历史学家与研究员，主要从事非洲研究。

22. 罗莎·卢森堡（1871—1919），波兰裔德籍马克思主义思想家，德国共产党前身的创始人。

23. 拉尔斯·马格努松（1952年生），瑞典乌普萨拉大学的经济历史学

家，在复兴霍布森学术研究方面发挥了重要作用。

24. 卡尔·马克思（1818—1883），德国政治哲学家，以《资本论》和《共产党宣言》等作品而著称。他的主要观点是人类社会通过阶级斗争实现从一个阶段向另一个阶段迈进，这构成了马克思主义思想的核心。

25. 约翰·米尔斯海默（1947年生），美国国际关系学教授和新现实主义思想家，他是"进攻性现实主义"的先驱人物，"进攻性现实主义"是对新现实主义的当代重新表述。

26. 纳撒尼尔·迈尔，英国记者、作家与左翼公共知识分子。

27. 艾伦·梅克辛斯·伍德（1942年生），美国马克思主义历史学家与学者，曾在加拿大约克大学任教。

28. 约翰·斯图尔特·密尔（1806—1873），英国自由主义哲学家和政治经济学家。他是早期主张"公民权利不受国家干预"观点的核心人物。"密尔"又译"穆勒"。

29. 阿尔伯特·马默里（1855—1895），英国商人和登山运动者。

30. 安东尼奥·内格里（1933年生），意大利马克思主义哲学家和政治煽动者。流亡法国期间在索邦大学任教，后于1997年返回意大利，因涉嫌参与叛国行动而被判入狱13年（由30年服刑期减为13年）。

31. 格雷戈里·诺埃尔，美国纽约州立大学的政治经济学教授，主要从事马克思主义和国际原油产业研究。

32. 托马斯·皮凯蒂（1971年生），法国经济学家和畅销书作者，以《21世纪资本论》著称，他在书中指出，从长期来讲，资本产生的收益要超过工人个人工资的收入。

33. 塞西尔·罗兹（1853—1902），南非的英国产业大亨与政治家。他创办了戴·比尔斯钻石公司，该公司目前占全球钻石贸易的40%。

34. 杰弗里·罗森（1964年生），美国法律学者，执教于耶鲁法学院。

35. 约翰·拉斯金（1819—1900），英国艺术批评家、社会思想家和慈善家。其论著《给这最后来的》（1860）主张在经济学思想中纳入社会因素。

36. 让-巴蒂斯特·萨伊（1767—1832），法国经济学家和商人，提出了萨伊定律。根据萨伊定律，生产带来了需求。该定律是古典经济学（一种反对政府干预经济的经济学理论方法）的一个准则。

37. 约瑟夫·熊彼特（1883—1950），奥地利经济学家和政治思想家，在多个领域均有著述。其最出名的著作主要研究创新与商业。他认为发明与"创造性毁灭"（比如马匹和马车被火车所取代）是经济发展的驱动力。

38. 亚当·斯密（1723—1790），苏格兰政治哲学家，被誉为经济学之父，其论著《国富论》（1776）创立了经济学这一学科。

39. 托斯丹·凡勃伦（1857—1929），美国经济学家、社会学家和制度经济学奠基人。制度经济学认为资本主义固有的历史遗存（制度）造成了资本主义效率低下。

40. 肯尼斯·华尔兹（1924—2013），美国国际关系学教授，主张重构现实主义使其更加科学（通常称为新现实主义）。

WAYS IN TO THE TEXT

KEY POINTS

- John Hobson (1858–1940) was an English economist and political thinker.

- Published in 1902, his book *Imperialism: A Study* argued that international aggression resulted from domestic economic conditions.

- Hobson was among the first to argue that a direct connection existed between inequality and aggressive foreign policy, and to further connect this to undue influence wielded by the wealthy and politically connected. This is as relevant now as it was to nineteenth-century England.

Who Was John Hobson?

John Hobson, the author of *Imperialism: A Study* (1902), was born in 1858 in the English county of Derbyshire and died in 1940. He studied Classics — that is, ancient Greek and Latin literature — at Oxford University, before beginning a career as a journalist. His family had been involved in the newspaper industry his entire life; indeed, his father owned one of Derbyshire's newspapers. He wrote for the *Manchester Guardian*, which in 1959 became the *Guardian*, a paper that remains globally important today. One of his most important jobs for the *Manchester Guardian* was to cover the Boer War,* a conflict between Britain and the descendants of Dutch settlers in what is today South Africa.

Hobson, a public intellectual, was a member of many famous "ethical" clubs in London and was associated with the socialist* Fabian Society,* which famously founded the London School of Economics (a prestigious seat of learning in London). While attending meetings of these societies, Hobson wrote many articles for liberal* weekly journals (that is, journals that shared his political beliefs about liberty and social justice). His experiences in southern Africa, and his work with the ethical societies, shaped his argument in *Imperialism*. More than just a liberal thinker, Hobson was an economist of some note as well. He and his friend Albert Mummery,* a businessman and mountain climber, wrote a book called *The Physiology of Industry* that was an important criticism of most economic theory at the time.

As he saw European nations turn from dominating the world to destroying one another in World War I,* his view of human nature became less economic and more personal; his experiences as a European public intellectual eventually led him to distrust human nature.

What Does *Imperialism* Say?

Hobson intended *Imperialism* to answer one main question: What is the rationale behind an imperial foreign policy — that is, a foreign policy aimed at empire building?

The consensus then was that conquering foreign lands would expand trade, thus enriching everyone — a belief summed up by the phrase "trade follows the flag." Hobson challenged this belief by showing that taking new land had no effect on trade and given that the British Empire was expensive to maintain in terms of both money and manpower, he looked for other explanations for the imperial project.

Hobson argued that the empire did make economic sense —

but only for a very small number of wealthy capitalists (that is, roughly speaking, investors and business owners). He came to this conclusion through a purely economic argument.

Hobson's theory of "oversaving," which he developed alongside his friend Mummery, held that some people kept too much money for themselves. This money was not reinvested into the economy, and more and more was held up in savings accounts. They reasoned that the rich would not invest it in things such as factories because many people were too poor to buy the things the factories made. The rich, then, bought things abroad, such as mines and railroads, as better investments. Since the wider world was not as safe as Britain, Hobson argued that rich people used their political connections to promote imperial policy.

Hobson thought that if wealth were redistributed, poor people would hold enough money at home that the rich could invest their money profitably without needing to look abroad. He called this redistribution "social reform" and based it on the idea of "social liberalism"* — the belief that organs of the state should guarantee the liberty of the citizen. This point of view emphasizes the rights of the community to live a good life, where their needs are met; government policy benefitting only a very few people was not only undemocratic, but also profoundly harmful to ordinary Britons.

There was also an important second part to this argument: the moral problems of imperialism,* the policy of subjugating territories abroad for economic gain.

Even if imperialism had no economic grounds, people still tried to justify it as a moral project on the grounds that Europeans were obliged to "civilize the savage." Hobson argued that arguments such as these were simply a cover for the economic ambitions of the empire, pointing out the ways in which imperialists chose domination over the process of civilization. This marked a key difference between "colonizing" (where the rights enjoyed by the civilized are extended to new lands) and "imperializing" (where one group is exploited by another outside its borders).

Imperialism did not only pose a problem for the dominated: for Hobson, imperial policy hurt British culture, too. He thought imperialism made British society more military — and that good soldiers, required to learn a forceful attitude where problems were solved by violence rather than dialogue, were not necessarily good citizens. Politicians who learned their trade in the empire, Hobson argued, were more likely to oppress citizens at home than those who learned in the UK.

Why Does *Imperialism* Matter?

According to Hobson, "financiers" — that is, people who make their living from investments — wield a disproportionate amount of power in the imperial project, although he does not adequately explain who, precisely, he means by this. Moreover, it can be argued that the line Hobson draws between capitalism* and imperialism is questionably straight. For students, then, the book provides an excellent case study of attractive but overly simple reasoning that does not, perhaps, take account of the complexity of the real world.

Although Hobson's theory was largely rejected by his peers,

Marxist* scholars turned to it, giving it some prominence. As people whose analysis of society was inspired by the theories of the economist and social theorist Karl Marx,* they agreed with Hobson that imperialism was bound to arise from capitalism (the economic system dominant today throughout the West and much of the developing world). They differed from Hobson, however, in their belief that the solution lay in revolution rather than reform.

Throughout the twentieth century, Hobson continued to influence political thinkers, inspired by his criticism of empire, but critics of imperial policy in the modern era bear little direct similarity to Hobson. Where he examined the role of a narrowly defined group of investors in perpetrating imperialism, political philosophers and thinkers such as the American literary theorist and philosopher Michael Hardt* and the Marxist philosopher Antonio Negri* consider imperialism as a kind of "state of mind." For them, imperialism is an idea that defines all social relations around the world — a great broadening of the term's use and implications.

Moreover, modern readers would look at Hobson's moral qualifications regarding imperialism with some skepticism; he believes, for example, that imperialism is moral when it involves "spreading civilization." Implying that one society is superior to another, this is no longer a persuasive argument.

While some of Hobson's ideas have fallen out of favor, the general direction of his theory remains much more important. *Imperialism*, read more generally, examines the connection between economic and political concerns. The politically and financially well connected can shape the world to their ends — and even though Hobson's argument does not prove this perfectly,the argument did help inspire a generation of scholars. Some of the most important twentieth-century theorists who followed in Hobson's footsteps were Marxists, who looked at the ways imperialism continues under different names. Hobson's arguments can give students a new perspective on the ways in which powerful countries acquired spheres of influence in the Cold War* (the period of tension between the Soviet Union and its allies and the United States and its allies in the years between 1947 and 1991).

Moreover, *Imperialism* can help readers learn to cast doubt on the justifications given to support foreign aggression; even if reading Hobson does not give us a coherent theory of *why* imperial policy occurs, it can give us a sense of *how* political statements spin reality into something that is not always as it seems.

SECTION 1
INFLUENCES

MODULE 1
THE AUTHOR AND THE HISTORICAL CONTEXT

KEY POINTS

* *Imperialism* retains its importance for study because it draws out moral and economic arguments for the economic rationale of international aggression.
* Hobson was a member of many left-wing societies, and worked as a journalist for left-wing newspapers covering the Boer War* (a British attempt to seize control of much of modern South Africa from the Boers — the descendants of Dutch settlers).
* European states engaged in a "scramble" for foreign lands in the nineteenth century.

Why Read This Text?

In his 1902 book *Imperialism: A Study*, the British economist and radical* reformer John Hobson argued that imperialism* — the policy of "empire building" in foreign territories — was a negative force both at home in Britain and in Britain's possessions abroad. Here, "radical" refers to a tradition in left-wing British politics committed to social justice through social reform.

Hobson's book stood out from other anti-imperialist writings because his argument was both ethical and economic. He set out not only to condemn imperial policy as immoral, but also to show that it was bad for the welfare of most citizens of the imperial state.

Contrary to the then popular assertion that "trade follows the flag" (meaning that extending Britain's empire meant extending

Britain's trade base as well, supposedly improving life for everybody),[1] Hobson argued that imperialism served to protect major capital investments abroad for the benefit of a "parasitic" class of ultra-wealthy financiers* at the taxpayer's expense.[2] Here, "capital investments" refers, simply, to money used to generate profit through investment — which is what financiers do for a living.

Hobson, who was to describe himself as an "economic heretic," should be remembered for his originality. *Imperialism* is no exception. "What was controversial at the time," wrote the British politician Jeremy Corbyn* in the introduction to the 2011 edition of *Imperialism*, "is his analysis of the pressures that were hard at work in pushing for a vast national effort in grabbing new outposts of empire."[3]

> *"What is attractive is Hobson's ability to separate and disassemble the interests of the commercial and imperial aims. He makes the valid point that other European countries, without the benefit of empires, manage to be successful trading and industrial powers in their own right."*
>
> ——Jeremy Corbyn, "Introduction," *Imperialism: A Study*

Author's Life

Hobson was born in 1858 to a middle-class family in the county of Derbyshire, England; his father was a prosperous newspaper owner. He started at Oxford University in 1876, where he read Classics (ancient Latin and Greek literature), although he developed an interest in philosophy and political economy* (a branch of the study of economics focused on the ways in which politics affects real economic outcomes) outside his studies.

On moving back to London, Hobson became a journalist and a lecturer; eventually he was sent to what is today South Africa to cover the Boer War,* a conflict fought in the years 1899–1902 between the British Empire and the descendants of Dutch settlers known as the Boers. As a journalist and something of a public intellectual, Hobson was a prolific writer of short essays and articles. *Imperialism* is, in fact, primarily an amalgamation of these articles, drawn from "diverse pieces written in 1901 and 1902, some in heavyweight academic journals, but most in less exacting liberal and radical weeklies like the *Speaker*."[4] "Liberal" here refers to a current in British politics that emphasizes the importance of individual liberty.

These articles were written in London in the war's immediate aftermath. Deeply influenced by what he saw in Africa, Hobson solidified his convictions that imperialism represented a devastating ploy foisted on the many by the ultra-wealthy.[5] Most of those in Hobson's immediate circle were defined by their long-standing membership in London's "ethical societies." These were groups of left-leaning intellectuals who would meet and discuss socialist* politics, philosophy, and economics.

Author's Background

The most important defining historical features of *Imperialism* are "late-stage" British imperialism more generally — a period of time often called the "scramble for Africa"* — and the Boer War specifically. In the 1890s, European powers were preoccupied with grabbing land in Africa; the Cambridge historian John Lonsdale* compares it to a horse race: "steeplechases into the far interior," focusing on the "forcible conversion of existing European predominance" into direct political control.[6]

The result of this competition between long-standing imperial powers (Britain and France) and newcomers to the imperial project (Belgium, Germany, and Italy) created a massive shift in African politics. It has been pointed out that "in 1879, more than 90 percent of the [African] continent was ruled by Africans," but by 1900, while Hobson was composing *Imperialism*, "all but a tiny fraction of it was being governed by European powers."[7]

Hobson's connection to the European scramble for Africa came primarily through his involvement in the Boer War as a correspondent for the *Manchester Guardian*. The British journalist, author, and left-wing intellectual Nathaniel Mehr* writes: "The British had been successful in subduing the settler population and asserting their political and economic supremacy over South Africa's lucrative mining regions, but the campaign, with its imprisoning of rural women and children, was widely considered to have been something of an embarrassing debacle, prompting much earnest soul searching among Britain's political establishment."[8]

Long before those leaders searched their souls, however, Hobson searched for their political and economic motivations.

1. John Hobson, *Imperialism: A Study* (Nottingham: Spokesman, 2011), 65.
2. Hobson, *Imperialism*, 85.
3. Jeremy Corbyn, foreword to *Imperialism: A Study*, by John Hobson (Nottingham: Spokesman, 2011), 7.
4. P. J. Cain, *Hobson and Imperialism: Radicalism, New Liberalism, and Finance: 1887–1938* (Oxford: Oxford University Press, 2002), 82.
5. Cain, *Hobson and Imperialism*, 92.
6. John Lonsdale, "The European Scramble and Conquest in African History," in *The Cambridge History of Africa*, vol. 6, *c. 1870 — c. 1905*, ed. Roland Oliver and G. N. Sanderson (Cambridge: Cambridge University Press, 1985), 681.
7. Roland Oliver and Anthony Atmore, *Africa since 1800* (Cambridge: Cambridge University Press, 2005), 118.
8. Nathaniel Mehr, "Introduction," in *Imperialism: A Study*, by John Hobson (Nottingham: Spokesman, 2011), 15.

MODULE 2
ACADEMIC CONTEXT

KEY POINTS

- The academic field of political economy* is concerned with examining the nature of wealth, and how societies can be made prosperous.
- Although liberal* political economists (that is, thinkers on economic matters who favored individual liberty) such as Adam Smith* and Jeremy Bentham* believed imperialism* was costly in terms of wealth, those such as John Stuart Mill* believed the value came from "civilizing" savage lands.
- While Hobson believed markets were usually imperfect, he agreed with classical liberal thinkers that imperialism — the policy of seizing foreign territory, generally with some kind of profit in mind — was expensive and immoral.

The Work in Its Context

John Hobson's *Imperialism: A Study* is a work of political economy: an academic tradition primarily concerned with, in the famous description of the English political philosopher John Stuart Mill, "the nature of Wealth, and the laws of its production and distribution: including, directly or remotely, the operation of all the causes by which the condition of mankind ... is made prosperous or the reverse."[1]

Political economy, in other words, looks at the relationship between wealth and society, and how different ways of producing wealth can create more or less prosperity. One of the most important conclusions to draw from Mill's statement is that the field of political economy is immersed in philosophy and ideas of how to distribute and produce the most value. Thus it is a much "wider" discipline than simply politics or economics.

Within the discipline, Hobson was profoundly influenced by the liberal tradition, which emphasized individual freedom and the idea that society could be made "rational." The tradition owes much to the influential English political theorist John Locke,* whose *Second Treatise of Government*, a foundational text for liberal thought, argued that government existed to protect private property.[2] Liberal political economists have a long history of criticizing imperialism; if government exists only to protect people's rights and property, then holding empires is surplus to requirements — and so, a waste of time and money.

> "In every department of human affairs Practice long precedes Science ... The conception, accordingly, of Political Economy as a branch of science is extremely modern; but the subject with which its enquiries are conversant has in all ages necessarily constituted one of the chief practical interests of mankind, and in some, a most unduly engrossing one. That subject is Wealth."
> —— John Stuart Mill, *Principles of Political Economy*

Overview of the Field

Hobson was deeply influenced by broadly conceived ideas of liberalism as defined by its great thinkers (notably the Scottish economist Adam Smith, the English philosopher and social reformer Jeremy Bentham, and the English political philosopher John Stuart Mill).

Liberalism and imperialism had an uneasy relationship from the start. Smith highlighted the costly nature of imperial mercantilism* (roughly speaking, trade encouraged by government policy) in his seminal book *Wealth of Nations*, writing that while empire "[raises] up a nation of customers, who should be obliged to buy from the shops of our different producers ... the home consumers have been burdened with the expense of maintaining and defending that empire," much to their detriment.[3] Bentham wrote of imperialism's moral problems: "[Give] up your colonies," he urged European statesmen, in a 1793 pamphlet entitled *Emancipate Your Colonies*, "because you have no right to govern them, because they had rather not be governed by you."[4]

By contrast, Mill complicated the standard liberal position, arguing that imperialism should be seen as a relationship of mutual benefit between Britain and her domains. Like Hobson after him, Mill believed that England had a surplus of population and capital (roughly, money available to be invested) that needed an outlet abroad through empire. Unlike Hobson, however, Mill believed empire to be a good solution and claimed not only that England's empire extended English liberalism throughout the so-called "unoccupied" lands of the world, but also that "the uncivilized dependencies also benefitted from the order and security, the investment and trade England provided."[5]

Despite their differences, all these thinkers are concerned with the relationship between prosperity and morality. In many ways, the political economy argument against imperial policy has usually been that it is both valueless, being very expensive and without benefit, and immoral, in terms of rights. Mill's justification of imperialism still fits this schema — except he argues that the morality of "civilizing" imperial subjects justifies the idea.

Academic Influences

Hobson's liberal thinking dates to his days at Oxford University, where his association with the liberal thinker T. H. Green* shaped his own broadly defined position as a "new"* (or "social"*) liberal:[6] he believed, that is, that the state has a role in ensuring personal liberty, notably by ensuring economic social justice.

Green is most famous for discussing the difference between "negative" liberty — a freedom from restriction, such as freedom of speech — and "positive" liberty, which is all about being enabled (being taught to speak, for example).[7] This was an important distinction between "classical" and "new" liberalism: classical liberalism emphasized freedom from government interference (negative liberty), whereas new liberalism focused on the obligation of individuals to help one another.

P. J. Cain,* one of Hobson's contemporary critics, wrote that new liberalism emphasized the rights of the community, rather than the individual, considering the individual flawed. This led new liberals to reject the perfect market of Say's Law,* which held that production is the source of all demand — that is, a worker will buy products with his or her income, in turn encouraging production in other areas.

Instead, new liberals viewed the market "as divisive, exacerbating poverty and threatening social collapse," and therefore wanting active control by the government.[8] This view was also broadly shared by two further great nineteenth-century liberals — John Ruskin* and Richard Cobden* — who inspired Hobson to such an extent that he would write their biographies.

Cobden was among the first, most strident voices to insist that imperialism was bad for England, writing: "It is ... an abiding conviction in my mind that we have entered upon an impossible and hopeless career in India."[9] Hobson took the standard liberal analysis of empire — that it is expensive and immoral — a step further by insisting that the imperial project was not just misplaced national fervor, but also the cynical plan of financiers* (people who profit from lending large sums of money to business ventures).

---

1. John Stuart Mill, *Principles of Political Economy with Some of Their Applications to Social Philosophy* (London: Longmans, 1865), 1.
2. John Locke, *Second Treatise of Government*, ed. C. B. Macpherson (Indianapolis, IN: Hackett, 1980), 20.
3. Adam Smith, *An Inquiry into the Nature and Causes of the Wealth of Nations* (London: Digireads, 2009), 391.
4. Jeremy Bentham, quoted in Bernard Porter, *Critics of Empire: British Radicals and the Imperial Challenge* (London: I. B. Tauris, 2007), 8.
5. Eileen Sullivan, "Liberalism and Imperialism: J. S. Mill's Defence of the British Empire," *Journal of the History of Ideas* 44, no. 4 (1983): 607–9.
6. P. J. Cain, *Hobson and Imperialism: Radicalism, New Liberalism, and Finance: 1887–1938* (Oxford: Oxford University Press, 2002), 21.
7. T. H. Green, "Liberal Legislation and Freedom of Contract," in *The Political Theory of T. H. Green: Selected Writings*, ed. John R. Rodman (New York: Meredith, 1964), 44–5.
8. Cain, *Hobson and Imperialism*, 21.
9. Richard Cobden, quoted in Porter, *Critics of Empire*, 13.

MODULE 3
THE PROBLEM

KEY POINTS
- The book's core question is "What is the economic rationale behind imperial foreign policy?"
- The debate was not an academic debate so much as a public debate; both inside and out of politics, attempts were made to justify imperialism on commercial grounds ("trade follows the flag") and moral grounds ("we are obliged to civilize the savage").
- Hobson and his fellow liberals* rejected both these claims. Hobson's counterargument was founded on a very tight scientific theory.

Core Question

With Europe's frantic scramble for Africa,* many political economists asked the question "What is the economic rationale behind this imperialist* foreign policy?" The common explanation of imperialist economics was mercantilist:* described by the assertion that "trade follows the flag," the basic idea of mercantilism is that the imperial nation needs raw materials for its industrial production at home and, therefore, requires territory abroad for two reasons. First, those territories supply the materials needed to manufacture products (which might be anything from clothing and furniture to guns) in the home country; second, once they are manufactured, these items get shipped out for purchase in the same colonies that provided the required materials in the first place. This point of view emphasizes that the most prosperous trade relations exist between a country and its own territories, meaning that imperialism is an economically sensible policy for the home country to follow.

Understandably, this idea had its critics. Many liberal thinkers, from Adam Smith* through Hobson, believed the mercantilism model was deeply flawed, and that imperialism was actually very expensive for Britain. The Boer War,* a conflict between the forces of the British Empire and the descendants of seventeenth-century Dutch settlers in what is today South Africa, represented a major moment for this question, and it is crucial to remember that Hobson had witnessed this debacle first hand. Hobson saw the apparent absurdity of imperialism, and his book attempted to understand why Britain might engage in such a mistaken venture. The wrongs committed in the name of the narrow interests of finance capitalism* — private profit made through private investment — were veiled in the discussion of a British struggle. Thus Hobson, among others, questioned imperial policy on both its economic and moral bases.

> *"This war [the Boer War] is a terrible disaster for everyone else in England and South Africa, but for the mine owners it means a large increase of profits from a more economical working of the mines, and from speculative operations."*
> ——John Hobson, *The War in South Africa*

The Participants

The debate between supporters and detractors of imperialism, as far as Hobson was concerned, did not occur like one staged in modern academia through journals or at universities. This debate was highly public, fought in the press and between the members of political parties.

The press was split between a majority of pro-war papers. As one historian puts it, "London journalists tended to portray the Boers as primitive and backwards ... They were often described in animal terms ... whose defeat by the superior civilization of the British was an inevitable result of social Darwinism"* — that is, roughly, as proof of the victors' inherent superiority and "evolutionary" advancement.[1] The domestic battleground was one of extreme patriotism,* where the war's critics were caricatured as "pro-Boer" or "anti-British"; Hobson dismissed the character of the debate as "jingoistic"* (by which he meant patriotic to an aggressive degree). His experiences were collected in his book *The War in South Africa*.[2]

This was not a simple public debate though. Hobson was a member of the Liberal Party,* a political party that sought the creation of a basic welfare state and a more secular society, and that valued individual freedom over conformity and tradition. But its members sitting in the British Parliament were divided on the imperial issue; those sympathetic to the Boers were united by a mutual condemnation of "the military methods used in the war as unnecessary and inhumane," notably the use of concentration camps,* but were not organized by any leadership. Their pro-war colleagues tended to overlook these issues because "Imperialism was the popular horse to ride."[3] Since these debates were fought in the political and not the academic arena, subtle compromises ensued. The origins of imperialism were not discussed; participants in the debate were interested in advancing dogmatic viewpoints, a humanitarian cause, or their own political careers.

The Contemporary Debate

Hobson's approach was quite different from that of his fellow Liberals in Parliament. A radical* (that is, someone who argued for social reforms designed to further the aims of left-wing liberalism),* he rejected these common views of imperialism, arguing that it was both immoral and unnecessarily expensive. Hobson was far from the only radical critic of imperialism, however. And nor was he the only one to accuse financiers* of being its chief instigators. Hobson's friend, the radical Scottish journalist J. M. Robertson, wrote, for example: "The primary object [of imperialism] is not to buy, but to sell, and receive goods in return to sell again; all to the end of heaping up more capital for investment."[4] Such attacks further entrenched anti-imperialism as a liberal cause. Yet what distinguished Hobson, in part, was his increased focus on finance capitalism. While many of Hobson's contemporaries (Robertson among them) argued that industry was central to imperialism, Hobson pointed to a particular group of people as being primarily responsible.[5]

Hobson, then, did not simply follow the classical liberals,* who were sympathetic to free trade and objected to imperialism on moral grounds alone, or follow the new liberals,* for whom intervention in the market was a moral position, in simply pointing the finger at the financiers' antisocial saving behavior as encouraging the imperial project.

Instead, he crafted a social scientific theory with testable conclusions that directly connected investment-based capitalism and imperialism — a vital contribution to the arguments of the anti-imperialist cause.

---

1. Kenneth Morgan, "The Boer War and the Media," *Twentieth Century British History* 13, no. 1 (2002): 5.
2. John Hobson, *The War in South Africa: Its Causes and Effects* (London: James Nisbet and Co. Ltd, 1900), 228.
3. John Auld, "The Liberal Pro-Boers," *Journal of British Studies* 14, no. 2 (1975): 93–4.
4. J. M. Robertson, *Patriotism and Empire* (London: Grant Richards, 1900), 172.
5. Peter Cain, "Radicalism, Gladstone and the Liberal Critique of Disraelian 'Imperialism,'" in *Victorian Visions of Global Order: Empire and International Relations in Nineteenth-Century Political Thought*, ed. Duncan Bell (Cambridge: Cambridge University Press, 2007), 226.

MODULE 4
THE AUTHOR'S CONTRIBUTION

KEY POINTS

- Hobson believed imperialism* was the direct result of finance capitalism* — that is, private investment made for the sake of private profit — and that inequality at home led to imperialism abroad.
- *Imperialism* sought to discredit claims that imperialism was profitable, while advancing the argument that it was an inevitable consequence of inequality.
- This argument was based on the theory of "underconsumption,"* according to which an economy will stagnate if there is not enough demand for products or services.

Author's Aims

John Hobson intended *Imperialism: A Study* to stand out from similar works by delivering a particularly devastating criticism of British imperial policy as a scheme of the ultra-wealthy financier* class. Imperialism, in other words, was a consequence of capitalism.

Hobson believed that imperialism resulted from domestic economic policy;[1] his goal was to provide an airtight, scientific theory that explained why massive inequalities in Britain created imperial policy abroad. He believed such a policy was in the interest of a few people of elite status — "financiers" who had accumulated so much capital that they could no longer profitably invest in Britain and wanted their investments abroad (such as gold mines and railroads) secured by military force.

Hobson intended his work to advocate for a policy change away from imperialism — which he saw as signifying the capture of the government by these financiers — toward social reform that included progressive taxation* (according to which taxation and earnings are linked), an increased minimum wage, and domestic redistribution programs to keep excess capital (profits, available for investment) at home, in the hands of consumers as wages.² Importantly, Hobson sought to arouse more than the British public's sense of decency (though he certainly argued against imperialism's immorality). He hoped to show how wealthy capitalists had defrauded them, and how it was in their best interests to reject imperialism.

> "It is idle to attack Imperialism or Militarism* as political expedients or policies unless the axe is laid at the economic root of the tree, and the classes for whose interest Imperialism works are shorn of the surplus revenues which seek this outlet."
>
> —— John Hobson, *Imperialism: A Study*

Approach

To win over his readers, Hobson did more than argue against the economic rationale of imperialism, or implicate financiers for promoting a policy that hurt everyone else. *Imperialism* is distinctive because Hobson's ideas combine to connect domestic wealth inequality in Britain with imperialist policy abroad, showing how one is the direct cause of the other. His theory is valuable because it does not just moralize, but generates testable predictions. That is to say, Hobson's theory predicts that a class of finance capitalists living in a state will eventually cause that state to pursue imperialist policy — it is merely a matter of when.

This very bold forecast was one of the principal factors that served to undermine the success of Hobson's theory.

Hobson built his opinions on an economic theory he proposed in *The Physiology of Industry* (1889), a book he wrote with the businessman Albert Mummery.* This theory was "underconsumptionism."

Whereas orthodox economics held that production and consumption always matched each other, Hobson believed this was a skewed view. "If a tendency to distribute income or consuming power according to needs were operative," Hobson wrote, "it is evident that consumption would ride with every rise of producing power." But this was not true; increased production did not match increased consumption, as finance capitalists* had amassed and retained so much wealth that most consumers lacked the means to do much purchasing. As a result of the underconsumption that followed, financiers sought productive use of their capital abroad.[3] They needed an empire to put their money to work in generating profit.

Contribution in Context

Hobson first linked imperial policy and underconsumption in his 1898 paper "Free Trade and Foreign Policy," in which he wrote: "Though a potential market exists within the United Kingdom for all 'goods' produced by the nation, there is not an 'effective' demand."[4]

Here, he is describing what occurs when the consumer has the desire to acquire goods but oversaving capitalists thwart his or her ability to spend, keeping money out of circulation, tied up in their enormous stockpiles.

These wealthy people "have not the desire," since "their material needs" would be satisfied with just a fraction of their money, while those "who have the desire have not the power."[5] In other words, wealthy people have more money than could possibly be useful to fulfill even their most lavish desires, while the poor have no way of getting enough to satisfy their basic needs because of an economic imbalance.

"Saving," Hobson and Mummery wrote in their *Physiology of Industry*, "increases the existing aggregate of capital, [but] simultaneously reduces the quantity of utilities and conveniences consumed." Any "excess" of saving, then, places too much capital in the hands of a few capitalists. This both reduces the value of capital and deprives ordinary people of access to money, preventing them from spending.[6]

---

1. John Hobson, *Imperialism: A Study* (Nottingham: Spokesman, 2011), 112.
2. Hobson, *Imperialism*, 108.
3. Hobson, *Imperialism*, 105.
4. John Hobson, "Free Trade and Foreign Policy," quoted in John D. Cunningham Wood and Robert D. Wood, *John A. Hobson: Critical Assessments of Leading Economists* (London: Routledge, 2003), XXXV.
5. Hobson, quoted in Wood and Wood, *John A. Hobson*, XXXV.
6. Albert Mummery and John Hobson, *The Physiology of Industry: Being an Exposure of Certain Fallacies in Existing Theories of Economics* (London: John Murray, 1889), VI–VII.

SECTION 2
IDEAS

MODULE 5
MAIN IDEAS

KEY POINTS

- Hobson's key themes are the political influence of the wealthy, the consequences of the economic stagnation caused by "underconsumption,"* and the social reform that was to solve these problems.
- Hobson's core argument is that consumption and production are not always in equilibrium, as finance capitalism* leads to underconsumption that throws off the balance between the two; finance capitalists exploit this imbalance to make and secure capital investments abroad; and imperialism* can be prevented with "social reform."
- Hobson's argument suffers from poor organization and a loose definition of the "financiers"* who are so important to his theory.

Key Themes

John Hobson's 1902 book, *Imperialism: A Study*, rests on a provocative overarching idea: the power of special interest groups — in this case, finance capitalists — to promote an imperialist policy in Britain. For Hobson, the wealthy finance capitalist is the "governor of the Imperial engine," because he possesses "those qualities of concentration and clear-sighted calculation which are needed to set Imperialism to work [in his favor]."[1]

This conclusion rests on a number of supporting arguments, including Hobson's theory of underconsumption, which consists of three sequential points:

- Excessive saving by the wealthy causes an oversupply of capital in industrial economies (that is, roughly, if the wealthy save rather than invest or spend, their money is tied up unproductively).
- This in turn creates a strong incentive for the wealthy to export that capital.
- This goal of exporting capital encourages them to influence foreign policy.

"Social reform," Hobson believed, was the key to ending imperialism; an equitable distribution of wealth would end the inequality produced by underconsumption and remove the incentive to seize lands abroad.

Hobson's argument assumes that although people are rational, inasmuch as they want to do what is best for themselves, they are fallible, because they can be tricked about what is actually best. This belief is core to his social liberalism* — a political philosophy founded on the idea that governments need to redistribute resources through social reform to ensure a positive outcome for all.

> "It is not industrial progress that demands the opening up of new markets and areas of investment, but mal-distribution of consuming power which prevents the absorption of commodities and capital within the country."
> —— John Hobson, *Imperialism: A Study*

Exploring the Ideas

The most important idea in Hobson's book is that finance

capitalism does not just encourage imperialism, it *causes* imperialism: "Imperialism is the endeavor of the great controllers of industry to broaden the channel for the flow of their surplus wealth by seeking foreign markets and foreign investments to take off the goods and capital they cannot sell or use at home."[2]

The root cause of this state of affairs, for Hobson, is "the maldistribution of capital within the country. The oversaving [of capital by the financier class] which is the economic root of Imperialism is found to consist of rents, monopoly profits, and other unearned or excessive elements of income."[3]

More importantly, this hoarded capital finds no use at home; though it exists in profound abundance, it largely rests outside the hands of actual consumers. Hobson believes that the need to "fight for foreign markets or foreign areas of investment" would disappear if the ultra-wealthy were not allowed to accumulate so much capital in the first place.[4]

This idea was notable because of the way it complicated Say's Law.* Named after the liberal* French economist Jean-Baptiste Say,* this law states that a paid producer of goods then purchases the production of others in a continuous economic cycle. As Hobson saw it, Say's Law could be contravened by oversaving; government intervention would then be needed to maintain equilibrium between consumption and production as a natural, orderly state of economic affairs.

Hobson's solution to the problem, then, is not to abandon imperialism: this would treat the symptom rather than the disease. Rather, Hobson advocated abandoning unregulated capitalism that allowed imperialism to arise in the first place. His solution was the redistribution of wealth through social programs, or social reform; through social reform, domestic inequality that leads to Britain's capital oversupply would be solved, and the financier class's massive incentive to encourage imperialism would be dismantled. Trade unions* (associations of laborers formed to protect the interests of working people) and socialism* (very roughly, a political philosophy founded on the idea that the government should intervene in the free market in order to protect society by ensuring a reasonably equitable distribution of wealth), both engines of social reform, "are thus the natural enemies of Imperialism, for they take away from the 'imperialist' classes the surplus incomes which form the economic stimulus of Imperialism."[5] In other words, Britain's foreign policy can only become ethical by confronting the imperialist leanings created by its domestic economy.

Language and Expression

A dominant theme — that oversaving by financiers leads them to advance their interests via imperialism — is generally expressed well in the first part of the book. Hobson presents his data clearly, often in table form, before discussing them and does not break off onto tangents. Despite this, it could be argued that the communication of the idea breaks down in two ways.

First, Hobson's overall theory rests on an assumption that he fails to prove or explore thoroughly: that the financier class possesses a near-perfect ability to direct "the patriotic forces" generated by "politicians, soldiers, philanthropists, and traders" into an imperialist policy that does not serve the interests of the people.[6] Hobson never makes clear, however, how these rich figures wield such control over the government.

Second, the latter half of the book leaves readers unclear as to whether financiers lead the imperialist drive, or follow the winds of foreign political expansion. Either they brandish "those qualities of concentration and clear-sighted calculation which are needed to set Imperialism to work," or "they simply and instinctively attach to themselves any strong, genuine elevated feeling ... and utilize it for their ends."[7] The apparently contradictory nature of Hobson's argument makes it difficult for the reader to decide which strategy dominates.

Hobson's key idea suffers because he treats the financier class as a kind of analytical dumping ground in his attempt to link causes and effects: they are not clearly enough defined and their powers are seemingly limitless. This problem has led critics to dismiss Hobson's work as a "conspiracy theory."[8]

---

1. John Hobson, *Imperialism: A Study* (Nottingham: Spokesman, 2011), 88.
2. Hobson, *Imperialism*, 106.
3. Hobson, *Imperialism*, 107.
4. Hobson, *Imperialism*, 107.
5. Hobson, *Imperialism*, 110.
6. Hobson, *Imperialism*, 88.
7. Hobson, *Imperialism*, 88, 191.
8. Nathaniel Mehr, "Introduction," in John Hobson, *Imperialism: A Study* (Nottingham: Spokesman, 2011), 29.

MODULE 6
SECONDARY IDEAS

KEY POINTS

- Hobson's moral argument against imperialism* is based on a distinction between "imperialism," which is exploitative, and "colonialism,"* which expands the nation; he also cautions against imperialism's threat to democracy at home.
- Hobson's secondary arguments, which refute the idea that imperialism is a moral good, are unconcerned with the economic effects of imperialism; that is another debate.
- Hobson's book is being re-examined in terms of capitalist institutions protecting themselves by eradicating alternatives around the world.

Other Ideas

The thrust of Hobson's main argument — that inequality at home leads to imperialism abroad — is supported by his more philosophical sub-argument. Hobson concerned himself with refuting the idea that imperialism was a beneficial international project and warned of the effects that excessive militarism* — a social tendency toward the exercise of military action, or a society reflecting a military model — would have on the British domestic situation. More imperialism abroad, he maintained, meant less liberal* democracy at home.

And while "imperialism" and "colonialism"* might seem to be words with identical meanings, Hobson draws an important distinction between the two by outlining the differences between the extension of national rights and the imposition of authority. Hobson defines nationalism* as "the establishment of a political community on the basis of nationality," and so colonialism merely extends that community — and the nation — through movement of citizens with full political rights to unpopulated lands. Imperialism, on the other hand, occurs "when a nation advances beyond the limits of nationality," and instead of governing fellow citizens with full rights, despotically possesses and exploits territory and people.[1]

Understanding the dissimilarities between "colonialism" and "imperialism" is crucial to understanding Hobson's moral argument about how British international projects ought to operate.

> *"There exists an absolute antagonism between the activity of the good citizen and that of the soldier. The end of the soldier is not, as is sometimes falsely said, to die for his country, it is to kill for his country."*
>
> —John Hobson, *Imperialism: A Study*

Exploring the Ideas

At a time when the "mission of civilization" was often touted as the moral purpose of imperialism, Hobson refuted this idea as part of his international argument. "In considering the ethics and politics of [imperial] interference," he wrote, "we must not be bluffed or blinded by critics who fasten on the palpable dishonesty of many practices of the gospel of the 'dignity of labour' and the 'mission of civilization.'"[2] The only legitimate interference with "lower races," Hobson believed, should work to bring them up to a state of rational self-government, and not exploit them in the interest of the civilizing country.[3]

This idea of imperialism as education to benefit the colonized dated back to the English liberal philosopher John Stuart Mill,* who saw four stages of societal development. These began with savagery and progressed to slavery and barbarism, "which is characterized, above all, by 'mental' shortcomings ... and 'positive defects of national character' making representative government impossible"; this was finally followed by modern liberal statehood.[4] He believed more developed nations must encourage the growth of those that lagged behind them.

Hobson, however, considered Mill's four steps as a moral cover for the profitable exploitation of the so-called "lower races," and that it would "preclude the genuine sympathy essential to the operation of the best civilizing influences."[5]

He also made a domestic argument against imperialism, charging that it promoted militarism and eroded democracy. "So far," Hobson wrote, "I have regarded the issue on its narrowly economic side. Far more important are the political implications of militarism [that] strike at the very root of popular liberty and the ordinary civic virtues."[6] Thus liberalism and militarism exist as opposite principles, "the one making for the evolution of the good citizen, the other for the evolution of the good soldier."[7]

In other words, good citizens have a social, cooperative attitude, while good soldiers have a dictatorial, forceful one. Hobson believed that when a soldier enters government, he will be more likely to command and oppress. Yet this critique of the imperial project as counter to liberalism was not original to Hobson. It had its origins among mid-nineteenth-century liberals such as the British statesman Richard Cobden,* who wrote: "It may seem Utopian, but I don't feel sympathy for a great nation, or for those who desire greatness of a people by vast extension of empire. What I like to see is the growth, development, and elevation of the individual man."[8]

Overlooked

The second part of Hobson's book focuses on the political concerns surrounding imperialism and is less often discussed than the first, which examines the economics of imperialism. The economic historian Lars Magnusson,* however, believes that increased focus on the neglected second part of the book does much to revitalize Hobson's theory. Most interpreters and critics of Hobson throughout the twentieth century focused only on his narrow economic explanation of imperialism, and it is popular to regard *Imperialism* as a prototype* for the book *Imperialism is the Highest Form of Capitalism*, a Marxist* analysis by the Russian revolutionary leader Vladimir Lenin.*

Magnusson, however, believes that economic explanations must always be set in the context of political ones, and that doing so shows Hobson as much more than a prototypical Lenin. He maintains that Hobson's real picture of "aggressive Imperialism after 1870" relied on "the emergence of theories of [social Darwinism],* including race theories, as well as the revival of increased nationalism and misguided patriotism."*9

In other words, Magnusson contends that a proper reading of Hobson gives as much weight to the second section of *Imperialism* as the first, and sees the economic explanation as only one part of a much more intricate theory that embraces history, politics, ideology, and economics.

Magnusson asserts that seeing Hobson in this way has major implications for how to perceive the entire book. For him, *Imperialism* "should rather be regarded as a precursor of modern institutional economics"* — that is, the study of how institutions and ideas shape economic behavior — "than merely a prototype of defunct Leninist* theory of Imperialism."*10

Magnusson also holds that the role of finance capitalists* in Hobson's theory is, in fact, relatively restricted and that his theory of imperialism should be seen as more similar to that of the American economist Thorstein Veblen.* "Imperialism," Veblen believed, "is dynastic politics under a new name, carried on for the benefit of absentee owners instead of absentee princes."[11] In the context of Magnusson's reappraisal, a striking similarity emerges between the ideas of Hobson and Veblen. For Hobson, institutions such as patriotism and racism play a pivotal, rather than a secondary, role, while Veblen relies on "patriotism ... as an additional explanatory variable [in] his theory of capitalism including its international dimension, imperialism."[12]

1. John Hobson, *Imperialism: A Study* (Nottingham: Spokesman, 2011), 45–8.
2. Hobson, *Imperialism*, 213.
3. Hobson, *Imperialism*, 214.
4. Beate Jahn, "Kant, Mill, and Illiberal Legacies in International Affairs," *International Organization* 59, no. 1 (2005): 194.
5. Hobson, *Imperialism*, 250.
6. Hobson, *Imperialism*, 142.
7. Hobson, *Imperialism*, 144.
8. Richard Cobden, quoted in Bernard Porter, *Critics of Empire: British Radicals and the Imperial Challenge* (London: I. B. Tauris, 2007), 14.
9. Lars Magnusson, "Hobson and Imperialism: An Appraisal," in *J. A. Hobson after Fifty Years*, ed. John Pheby (London: Macmillan, 1994), 156.
10. Magnusson, "Hobson and Imperialism," 160.
11. Thorstein Veblen, *Absentee Ownership and Business Enterprise in Recent Times* (New York: Kelley, 1964), 35.
12. Stephen Edgell and Jules Townshend, "John Hobson, Thorstein Veblen, and the Phenomenon of Imperialism: Finance Capital, Patriotism, and War," *American Journal of Economics and Sociology* 51, no. 4 (1992): 412.

MODULE 7
ACHIEVEMENT

KEY POINTS

- Although Hobson's "scientific" theory of imperialism* itself did not have lasting impact, the general thrust of his thought has retained importance.
- Imperialism remained a force in the twentieth century, and Hobson remained relevant to the study of this phenomenon.
- *Imperialism* maintains a complicated relationship with issues of race: Hobson implicated Jewish people in perpetrating imperialism.

Assessing the Argument

While *Imperialism: A Study* retains a great deal of importance, John Hobson did not quite accomplish his key goal of establishing a direct causal chain between inequality and imperialism. Hobson is prone to "conceptual slippage," meaning that his analysis of imperialism appears contradictory; certain concepts become narrower and broader as he writes. One of the best examples of this slippage involves Hobson's idea of capitalists* who act as the governing force of imperialism, and whether they believe their own jingoism* (that is, aggressive love of one's country).

In the first part of the book, imperialists are cynical financiers,* motivated only by their investment needs as they seek to manipulate a credulous Britain into pursuing a destructive imperialist policy.[1] Later in the book, however, when discussing the psychological power of imperialism, Hobson admits a good deal more emotion and patriotism* to the financier class: "Imperialist politicians, soldiers, or company directors who push a forward policy by portraying the cruelties of the African slave raids ... do not deliberately and consciously work up these motives in order to incite the British public. They simply and instinctively attach to themselves any strong, genuine elevated feeling ... and utilize it for their ends."[2]

If Hobson did not realize his goal of providing a universal discrediting of imperial policy, it is because of this conceptual slippage. Although the "financier class" is of critical importance to his theory, his definition of that class changes as his argument develops; this may, however, be a consequence of the fact that *Imperialism* was not composed as a single work, but was produced from a number of cobbled-together papers.

> "One must, however, insist again that Hobson's lasting contribution is his psychological analysis of imperialism. He was at his best in laying bare the roots of man's infinite capacity for self-deception, for man naturally seeks some ethical underpinnings for his approval of policies he would ordinarily condemn at home."
>
> —— Harvey Mitchell, "Hobson Revisited,"
> *Journal of the History of Ideas*

Achievement in Context

In his eagerness to create a universally applicable "theory" of imperialism akin to science, Hobson may have overstated his case. He wrote that maldistribution of wealth in one country leads to global imperialism as fire leads to smoke, but in reality it is difficult to make these absolute arguments in the complex realm of society. This explains in large part why his work met with a lukewarm reception among his fellow liberals* and was virtually ignored by the general public early on. More sympathetic interest in Hobson's theory arose later — first in the Marxism* of the Russian communist leader Vladimir Lenin* and later in the 1960s, as interest in the study of imperialism grew in the context of the Cold War* (a 44-year period of tension between the United States, the Soviet Union,* and the nations aligned around them).

The focus of imperialism shifted from Britain to America and, during the Cold War, the Soviet Union. Renewed interest in the study of imperialism, as Michael Barratt Brown* wrote in the introduction to *The Economics of Imperialism*, "certainly reflects widespread dissatisfaction with narrowly political explanations [of imperial activity], in terms of 'defending the free world' or 'rescuing the achievements of communism,'* respectively, for what the United States has been doing in the Caribbean and Southeast Asia and the Soviet Union in Eastern Europe."[3]

Limitations

Imperialism has endured criticisms of anti-Semitism* (anti-Jewish sentiment) and Eurocentrism* (a world view that prioritizes the pre-eminence and assumptions of Europe and European people).

The former comes from Hobson's line that the financier class in supposed control of imperial policy consists mainly of "men of a single and peculiar [Jewish] race, who have behind them many centuries of financial experience."[4] Anti-Semitism was common in

Hobson's political circles, and he was ultimately seen as the victim of a popular stereotype that located "responsibility for the [Boer] War* ... [in] the unworthy motives of Jewish financiers."5

While he indicted Jews as responsible for capitalism,* this did not form a major part of his argument, and this belief has not changed the way Hobson is seen today. His more extended treatment of the "lower races" as children needing guidance, however, is much more controversial in a modern context. The conclusion that white interference in non-white society is necessary as a "civilizing mission" forms the basis for Hobson's justification of a "benign" or "sane" imperialism.6

This picture poses problems, as the Canadian international relations professor David Long* points out. First, Hobson fails to recognize that these societies were perfectly able to govern themselves without white interference. Secondly, Hobson's problem with imperialism is "not with [the] notion of control over subject peoples but rather the competition among the Western nations for control, that is, as bad fathers or bad teachers."7 This vein of criticism has made Hobson's call for "sane" imperialism less valid, and reveals that his vision of capitalism, even if inspired by perceived injustice, lacked pinpoint focus.

---

1. John Hobson, *Imperialism: A Study* (Nottingham: Spokesman, 2011), 86.
2. Hobson, *Imperialism*, 191.
3. Michael Barratt Brown, *The Economics of Imperialism* (London: Penguin, 1974), 17–18.
4. Hobson, *Imperialism*, 86.

5. Harvey Mitchell, "Hobson Revisited," *Journal of the History of Ideas* 26, no. 3 (1965): 400.
6. Hobson, *Imperialism,* 216.
7. David Long, "Paternalism and the Internationalization of Imperialism: J. A. Hobson on the International Government of the 'Lower Races,'" in *Imperialism and Internationalism in the Discipline of International Relations*, ed. David Long and Brian Schmidt (Albany: University of New York Press, 2005), 87.

MODULE 8
PLACE IN THE AUTHOR'S WORK

KEY POINTS
- Hobson's main focus was on tying economic theories to political outcomes, though he focused mostly on politics later in life.
- Hobson's later work ignored the economic justifications of imperialism* and concentrated more on human nature.
- Hobson's work was dismissed in his lifetime; even the economist John Maynard Keynes,* who admired Hobson, found his writing style confusing and the quality variable.

Positioning

John Hobson's *Imperialism: A Study* came about in the midst of an extremely prolific career. While it is usually (though not exclusively) lauded as his most enduring work of importance, it was neither his first major treatise on economics, nor his first on imperialism.

Hobson's first major work, co-written with British businessman Albert Mummery* in 1889, was *The Physiology of Industry*, where he outlined the underconsumption theory* that would provide the theme for most of his subsequent work. *Imperialism* was not Hobson's first anti-imperialist work. His 1898 article "Free Trade and Foreign Policy" outlined his theory of economic imperialism, tying underconsumption theory to imperial expansion, and proposing domestic reform as a peaceful, desirable alternative. In the article, he drew a sharp distinction between imperialism and the "internal social and industrial reforms" required to achieve an even distribution of wealth.[1] Hobson would go on to provide evidence for this theory in *Imperialism*.

He later moderated his extreme position, writing in his autobiography, *Confessions of an Economic Heretic*, that "by enlisting my combative instincts in defence of my heretical views of capitalism as a source of unjust distribution, oversaving, and an economic impulse to adventurous imperialism, it led me for a time to an excessive and too simple advocacy of the economic determination of history."[2] In this later period of Hobson's life — *Heretic* was published two years before his death in 1940 — he adopted a much more general view of imperialism: he believed it resulted from the natural acquisitiveness and assertiveness of human beings rather than any particular economic system.

> *"By enlisting my combative instincts in defence of my heretical views of capitalism as the source of unjust distribution, oversaving, and an economic impulse to adventurous imperialism, it led me for a time to an excessive and too simple advocacy of the economic determination of history."*
> — John Hobson, *Confessions of an Economic Heretic*

Integration

While largely focused on the theme of underconsumption and concerned with imperial expansion, Hobson's body of work was not necessarily unified. For example, Hobson's very earliest work on imperialism was not anti-imperialist, and he did not remain convinced of his own conclusions as his career continued past *Imperialism*. This is evident in his 1911 article "An Economic Interpretation of Investment," where he softened his previous position, writing that the international character of many investment cartels removes the "temptation or ... ability" of financiers* to manipulate states into imperial policies.³

In the wake of World War I,* however, Hobson was filled with renewed pessimism as to whether economic interdependence could supplant militarism* (the belief that a nation's aims can be achieved by military action) in developed nations. This led him first to reduce the role of financiers and increase the role of politicians in promoting foreign militarism in his 1917 book *Democracy after the War*. Then, in his 1926 book *Free Thought in the Social Sciences*, he concluded that "Imperialism is mainly the expression of two dominant human instincts, self-assertion and acquisitiveness."⁴ But *Free Thought* also represents a widening of Hobson's scope of inquiry as he considers the nature of the social sciences themselves — and of man in society — rather than a particular social phenomenon.

Now more interested in how psychology can be folded into the field of political economy, Hobson identifies human nature as the independent cause of imperialism, and explains that his original economic explanation only masked this fact. From this time on, he became more interested in social theories in general, rather than theories of any narrow phenomenon. Still, a single characteristic unites all of Hobson's work: his preoccupation with how government intervention, and the redistribution of wealth in particular, can improve the lives of all.

Significance

Hobson's body of work has had mixed fortunes overall; outside "small coteries of friends, admirers, and like-minded social critics," he did not have a wide impact on political thought until some years later.[5] Yet subsequent thinkers, including the Russian leader Vladimir Lenin* and the English economist John Maynard Keynes,* have credited Hobson as a direct inspiration. However, he was also a flawed one, as Keynes noted when he assessed the mixed power of Hobson's body of work in 1914: "One comes to a new book by Mr. Hobson with mixed feelings," he wrote, "in hope of stimulating ideas and some fruitful criticisms of orthodoxy from an independent and individual standpoint, but expectant of much sophistry, misunderstanding, and perverse thought."[6]

This general observation reflects the view of Hobson's argument in *Imperialism* as profoundly insightful but ultimately flawed. Yet because of its insight, *Imperialism* has enjoyed continued influence around the world, especially when the Cold War* ignited an international power struggle between the United States and the Soviet Union.* Once again, critics of empire referred back to Hobson to wonder whether the international escapades of the two superpowers were actually driven by narrow economic interests.

Those critics were not necessarily "Hobsonites," however, as they did not share Hobson's theory and its strong claims, sharing instead his general suspicion of wealthy countries pursuing international military projects.

1. John Hobson, quoted in P. J. Cain, *Hobson and Imperialism: Radicalism, New Liberalism, and Finance: 1887–1938* (Oxford: Oxford University Press, 2002), 75.
2. John Hobson, *Confessions of an Economic Heretic* (Hassocks: Harvester Press, 1976), 63.
3. John Hobson, quoted in Michael Schneider, *J. A. Hobson* (London: Macmillan, 1996), 102.
4. Schneider, *J. A. Hobson*, 103.
5. Michael Freeden, *Reappraising J. A. Hobson* (London: Unwin Hyman, 1990), 3.
6. John Maynard Keynes, "Review of *Gold, Prices, and Wages*," *Economic Journal* 23 (1913): 393.

SECTION 3
IMPACT

MODULE 9
THE FIRST RESPONSES

KEY POINTS

- *Imperialism*, upon publication, was either ignored or dismissed for failing to prove its "conspiracy theory" of perfect control by financiers.*
- Hobson responded by trying to tie his "conspiracy theory" to real figures — exaggerating the role of Cecil Rhodes,* for example.
- *Imperialism* was never popular for its theory, but rather for its argument that imperial policy was irrational. When the Cold War* renewed debate about imperial policy, *Imperialism* was once again part of the conversation.

Criticism

Imperialism: A Study had little immediate impact outside the immediate circle of John Hobson's fellow radicals.* As a result, the first criticisms Hobson endured did not come from conservatives or pro-imperialists, but from fellow liberals* who believed he overstated his case. "Even amongst some of the Liberals and Radicals who agreed with Hobson," writes the British history professor P. J. Cain,* *Imperialism* was ignored because it was seen to "absurdly overstate" the evils of imperialism.*[1]

The English author Norman Angell,* writing under the pseudonym Ralph Lane, was one of Hobson's more prominent critics. He pointed out that Hobson imbued the financier class with a near-superhuman ability to influence policy — and with near-inhuman detachment. "The intensity of feeling," Angell wrote, "which embraced ... the whole nation — a feeling which in every characteristic was non-rational — precludes the idea that it had its origins or is mainly animated by a limited clique whose motives are intensely rationalistic."[2]

This criticism of the conspiracy theory damaged Hobson's case, and its ill-defined stereotype of an all-powerful financier class would plague it. Even *Imperialism*'s most favorable newspaper review was far from flattering. The *Edinburgh Review* agreed with Angell that it was preposterous to suppose that British policy was dictated by "self interested groups of financiers and millionaires," and that these exaggerations concealed from readers the underlying power and appeal of its argument against imperial policy.[3]

> "Hobson's sinister capitalists and their 'parasites' were nothing more than a hypothesis, a *deus ex machina*, to balance an equation between the assumed rationality of mankind and the unreasonableness of imperial policies: and the book was a plea for a return to a sane standard of values. His mistake, then, was to think that the equation needed such artificial adjustment."
> —— D. K. Fieldhouse, "*Imperialism*: An Historiographical Revision," *Economic History Review*

Responses

Though Hobson reissued *Imperialism* in 1905, he altered the text very little. The British historian P. J. Cain gives a list of his alterations: "Hobson tried to strengthen his claims about the weak association between foreign trade growth and recent Imperial expansion," and he reclassified South Africa as a "tropical" (meaning non-white) territory as opposed to a "white-settled" one (akin to Australia or Canada). Ultimately, though, he left his core argument largely unaltered.[4]

While not a direct response to his critics, Hobson reissued his first major work, *The Evolution of Modern Capitalism*, in 1906, just a year after reissuing *Imperialism*. In this printing of *Capitalism*, Hobson wrote a new chapter laying out the general power of the financier class in a more concrete way than *Imperialism* did, focusing on the British tycoon and statesman Cecil Rhodes: "The most distinctive feature of South African finance has been the skilled use which the financiers have made of political machinery to assist them in improving and marketing investments. The actual lands which form the material basis of industrial and speculative exploitation ... have in each case involved in their acquisition the application of a medley of non-economic forces, legal treachery ... and diplomatic coercion."[5]

While Hobson pointed to the success of the financiers, and their propensity to fiddle in politics, he still did not fix the break in his line between financial capitalism and imperialism. So the question remained: how, specifically, do financiers wield such comprehensive power to write policy?

Conflict and Consensus

Critical debate around *Imperialism* was largely unproductive, and nothing resembling a fruitful academic discourse emerged until later in the twentieth century. By this time, the conspiracy elements of Hobson's theory were dropped in favor of a more complex set of relationships between state and finance interests.

Of the criticisms Hobson endured in the twentieth century, the one from the historian D. K. Fieldhouse,* a specialist in the British Empire, was the most thorough. "Hobson's own claim to importance and originality lies simply in his having introduced British, and subsequently world, opinion to accept his special definition of the word Imperialism."[6] This definition held that imperialism was a kind of degenerate, exploitative endeavor in the narrow capitalist* interests of the imperialist state. Fieldhouse believed that Hobson's economic theory of imperialism, and its focus on finance capitalists,* was "a pamphlet for the times, rather than a serious study of the subject ... [owing] much of its success to the fact that it expressed a current idea with peculiar clarity, force, and conviction."[7]

Ultimately, Fieldhouse found Hobson's economic theory unsound because it failed to explain capital export properly: "Detailed investigations have shown that the alleged needs of the European investor ... to find outlets for his surplus capital had little or nothing to do with the division of Africa and the Pacific between the European powers." Moreover, imperial expansion after 1870 resulted from the need to protect existing possessions, and "on the economic side," motivations were largely unchanged.[8]

Yet having established these points, Fieldhouse believes that Hobson's analysis had one major valuable aspect: it asserted that imperialism was largely irrational. Since Hobson could not accept this at face value, he had to invent a conspiracy of financiers for whom it was rational — figures who Fieldhouse believed were "a hypothesis ... to balance an equation between the assumed rationality of mankind and the unreasonableness of imperial policies."⁹

---

1. P. J. Cain, *Hobson and Imperialism: Radicalism, New Liberalism, and Finance: 1887–1938* (Oxford: Oxford University Press, 2002), 163–4.
2. Norman Angell, quoted in Cain, *Hobson and Imperialism*, 118–9.
3. Timo Särkkä, *Hobson's Imperialism: A Study in Late Victorian Political Thought* (Jyväskylä: University of Jyväskylä, 2009), 166.
4. Cain, *Hobson and Imperialism*, 171–2.
5. John Hobson, *The Evolution of Modern Capitalism* (London: The Walter Scott Publishing Company, 1906), 266.
6. D. K. Fieldhouse, "Imperialism: An Historiographical Revision," *Economic History Review* 14, no. 2 (1961): 187.
7. Fieldhouse, "Imperialism," 189.
8. Fieldhouse, "Imperialism," 213.
9. Fieldhouse, "Imperialism," 214.

MODULE 10
THE EVOLVING DEBATE

KEY POINTS

- Hobson's *Imperialism* helped inaugurate debates on the relationship between economic interests at home and political aggression abroad, and dismissed arguments about trade and racial ethics.

- Marxist* thinkers such as Vladimir Lenin* and the Polish German activist Rosa Luxemburg* took Hobson's ideas and extended them to call for revolution rather than reform; modern Marxist thinkers such as Ellen Meiksins Wood* and David Harvey* investigate informal "covert" imperialism.*

- Post-Marxists* (thinkers who reject certain principles that are key to Marxist theory), such as the American political theorist Michael Hardt* and the Italian philosopher Antonio Negri,* argue that the empire of the twenty-first century is not dominated by one power but is rather a "state of affairs" where capitalism* itself dominates everywhere.

Uses and Problems

Hobson's core idea — the relationship between militarism,* capitalism, and imperialism — was developed by his fellow theorists of imperial power during the early twentieth century.

The most famous Marxist theorist attracted by Hobson's indictment of capitalist imperialism was Vladimir Lenin,* the first communist* premier of the Soviet Union.* Echoing Hobson, Lenin wrote: "Imperialism is the monopoly stage of capitalism ... in which the export of capital has acquired pronounced importance."[1]

The chief difference between the two thinkers involved the cure for imperialism: Hobson held that the crisis could be overcome through redistribution, while Lenin believed that the only way to get rid of imperialism was to get rid of capitalism altogether.

And while the Austrian economist and political thinker Joseph Schumpeter* agreed that economic and military forces figured in imperialism, he turned Hobson's thesis on its head. Whereas Hobson believed that economic considerations in turn bred militarism, Schumpeter theorized that imperialism was rooted in militarism, with economic justifications applied after the fact. "Created by wars that required it, the [state war machine] now created the wars it required" by manufacturing economic justifications.[2] Schumpeter and Hobson agreed, however, on the illiberal* ramifications of militarism (that is, the consequences that compromised individual liberty).

The German political thinker Hannah Arendt* took this idea further, reemphasizing the ethical argument in her seminal work *The Origins of Totalitarianism*, where she wrote that imperialism resulted from the spread of capitalist thinking (and specifically the pursuit of unlimited growth) in the public sphere; that "expansion as a permanent and supreme aim of politics is the central idea of Imperialism."[3] Crucially for Arendt, the ideology of permanent expansion violated ethical and moral limits on politics — which echoed Hobson's concerns that imperial policy abroad damaged liberal* politics at home.

> "We should emphasize that we use 'Empire' here not as a metaphor ... but rather as a concept, which calls primarily for a theoretical approach. The concept of Empire is characterized fundamentally by a lack of boundaries: Empire's rule has no limits. First and foremost, then, the concept of Empire posits a regime that effectively encompasses the spatial totality, or really that rules over the entire 'civilized' world. No territorial boundaries limit its reign."
>
> —— Michael Hardt and Antonio Negri, *Empire*

Schools of Thought

Hobson's scientific approach in *Imperialism* has attracted Marxists throughout history. While they agreed in general that capitalist excess intertwined with imperialism, they disagreed on the root causes and cures for that overall condition. The Marxists were deterministic, believing that capitalism was an inevitable stage of history, with imperialism the final stage of capitalism. Thus a violent overthrow of capitalism and a cure for imperialism were the same thing — a sharp contrast to Hobson's appeal for a friendlier, equal form of capitalism.

The Polish German Marxist thinker Rosa Luxemburg based her theory of imperialism on the idea that "the colonial (developing) countries required finance from the capitalist countries for development in order to create markets for those capitalist countries."[4] Capitalism, in other words, will always need to open new markets to maintain profitability, meaning that capitalist states will fight over non-capitalist countries — "but the more violently, ruthlessly, and thoroughly Imperialism brings about the decline of non-capitalist civilizations, the more rapidly it cuts the ground from under the feet of capitalist accumulation."[5] Imperialism, in other words, is not just about exporting capital, but also about making more societies capitalist.

Late twentieth-century Marxists, especially the British social geographer David Harvey and the Canadian historian Ellen Meiksins Wood, contest the role of the state in imperial policy. They argue that while modern imperialism is largely non-territorial and non-expansionary, it relies on state hegemony* (or dominance) and the constant threat of military action.[6] Power defines "asymmetries of exchange relations [between more and less developed nations] ... forcing open markets throughout the world by institutional pressures exercised through ... [financial institutions such as the International Monetary Fund* and the World Bank]* backed by the power of the United States ... to deny access to its own vast market."[7]

In Current Scholarship

The two most famous post-Marxist critics of empire are Michael Hardt and Antonio Negri. For both of them, the "Empire" is a globalized system defined by capitalism, but without a national center. The capitalist system benefits and awards privileges to some nation states over others (for example, the United States as compared with the developing world), but has also emerged as a network of international organizations such as the International Monetary Fund and the World Bank, transnational corporations, and social connections between the powerful.

In Hobson's thinking, capital propelled the nation state to do its bidding; in Hardt and Negri's thinking, capital has *superseded* the nation state. "The concept of Empire," they write, "is characterized fundamentally by a lack of boundaries: Empire's rule has no limits."[8] First, they argue, this means that empire encompasses the entire world; second, empire is no longer imposed by any one state, but is instead a "state of affairs"; and finally, "Empire operates on all registers of the social order extending down to the depths of the social world."[9] In their paradigm or model, the power of globalized* (worldwide) capitalism is not controlled by some powerful individuals at the expense of others, but is so powerful in and of itself that it controls the entire world's population of both "exploiters" and "exploited" by defining who they are and how they relate to one another.

In essence, Hardt and Negri have moved away from a number of Hobson's core ideas, such as the one-way relationship where capitalists and statesmen oppressed imperial subjects, and emphasize instead the ever-increasing power of capitalism. In Hobson, capitalism defined state policy; in Hardt and Negri, the ascent of capitalism is complete, and it has come to define everything, everywhere.

---

1. Vladimir Lenin, *Imperialism: The Highest Stage of Capitalism* (New York: International Publishers, 1939), 88–9.

2. Joseph Schumpeter, *Imperialism and Social Classes: Two Essays*, trans. Heinz Norden (New York: Meridian, 2007), 25.
3. Hannah Arendt, *The Origins of Totalitarianism* (New York: Harcourt, 1968), 125.
4. Philip Arestis and Malcolm Sawyer, *The Elgar Companion to Radical Political Economy* (Aldershot: Edward Elgar, 1994), 21.
5. Rosa Luxemburg, *The Accumulation of Capital*, accessed February 22, 2014, http://www.marxists.org/archive/luxemburg/1913/accumulation-capital/ch31.htm.
6. Ellen Meiksins Wood, *Empire of Capital* (London: Verso, 2005), 130.
7. David Harvey, *The New Imperialism* (Oxford: Oxford University Press, 2005), 32.
8. Michael Hardt and Antonio Negri, *Empire* (Cambridge, MA: Harvard University Press, 2000), xv.
9. Hardt and Negri, *Empire*, xv.

MODULE 11
IMPACT AND INFLUENCE TODAY

KEY POINTS

- Hobson is no longer an "active" participant in today's debates — he is more important for his insight into the way private interests can subvert the state.
- According to neorealist* theories explaining international relations (that is, the interactions of nations), all foreign aggression by states results from rational power calculation; the social theorists David Harvey* and Ellen Meiksins Wood* respond by suggesting that the Iraq War* was politically irrational but economically sensible.
- According to neorealist theories of international relations, no state would take the chance of pursuing economic gains through war, as it is simply too risky; the United States fights abroad to reshape the world in its own image and guarantee its security.

Position

John Hobson's 1902 book *Imperialism: A Study* is no longer an active part of the current economic or political debate. In general, Hobson's role is appreciated less for his theory in itself than for his having inaugurated criticism of imperialism* as an economic, rather than a political, phenomenon that is in the interests of a minority.

The American economist Gregory Nowell's* treatment of Hobson gives an example of why this is so: "Are we still talking about Hobson? Yes and no. Hobson's core issues are oligarchy* [government by a minority], oligopoly* [the hold on a market by a small number of producers], their impact on the political system, their impact on the potential for social control over investment, and redistribution of income. This," Nowell writes, "is the true Hobson, who appeals to the modern reader, not the narrowly construed explicator of colonialism."*1

So while important for the study of history, and the history of ideas, Hobson's analysis of British imperialism is incidental to the perspectives of politics and economics — and this limits his analysis of capitalist* power.2 Modern Marxists* such as David Harvey and Ellen Meiksins Wood reject Hobson's "conspiracy theory" in favor of a more general presumption that the interests of American enterprise and government are roughly aligned.3 Both Harvey and Meiksins Wood take their inspiration from Hobson by analyzing the connection of military activity and capitalist expansion: "Boundless domination of a global economy," writes Meiksins Wood, "and of the multiple states that administer it, requires military action without end, in purpose or time."4 In that spirit, both writers agree that imperialism is connected to the requirement of "global hegemony"* (that is, a dominant force), initiated either by a capitalist power (Harvey), or by a group of states in support of capitalism generally (Meiksins Wood).

> "The building blocks of Hobson's Imperialism were then and are now relevant for understanding capitalism."
>
> ——Gregory Nowell, "Hobson's *Imperialism*,"
> *The Political Economy of Imperialism*

Interaction

In his book *Theory of International Politics* (1979), the American political theorist Kenneth Waltz* offered a very critical analysis of Hobson's argument as he made the case for the neorealist school of thought.

Neorealism asserts that state action can always be understood in terms of relative power; that is, states try to maximize their power relative to other states, and powerful states pursue regional hegemony (dominance) as an end in itself.[5] These theorists would see post-Cold War* American dominance of global politics as an example of this.

In other words, neorealist thought, as set out by Kenneth Waltz and updated by the political theorist John Mearsheimer* in his book *The Tragedy of Great Power Politics* (2001), is a persuasive challenge to Hobson's analysis.

More recent theorists of imperial power, however, have responded to the neorealist idea that foreign conflict is driven by state security interests. David Harvey, for example, would counter that the neorealist position is mistaken to dismiss the invasion of Iraq as irrational, arguing that it was rational from a narrow, economic point of view.

"When Joseph Chamberlain* led Britain into the Boer War* ... at the beginning of the twentieth century," Harvey writes, "it was clear that gold and diamond reserves were the prime motivation." In turn, this would allow over-accumulated capital in Britain to be invested abroad.[6] Likewise, "the drive of the administration [of

President George W. Bush*] to intervene militarily in the Middle East," he argues, "has to do with procuring firmer control over Middle Eastern oil resources ... [and] the general lowering of oil prices can be seen as one tactic in seeking to confront the chronic problems of over-accumulation that have arisen over the past three decades."[7]

Harvey argues that the Iraq War, like Hobson argued for the Boer War, was rational from the point of view of finance capitalism,* but irrational from the point of view of both public and strategic interests.[8]

Meiksins Wood contends that America's "economic empire would be sustained by political and military hegemony over a complex state system," concerned especially with opening a "third world that had to be made available to Western capital."[9] She also outlines her differences with Harvey's view of capitalist imperialism, saying "he argues that ever-expanding capital accumulation must be accompanied by an ever-expanding political power and command over territory, and that this is the logic of capitalist imperialism. I argue almost the reverse: the specificity of capitalist imperialism lies in the unique capacity of capital to impose its hegemony *without* expanding its territorial political power ... Capitalism alone has created an autonomously *economic* form of domination."[10]

The Continuing Debate

Neorealism has challenged Hobson and the contemporary Marxists since its inception; in fact, Kenneth Waltz used *Imperialism* as an example of an incorrect theory. Waltz argued that many different kinds of states, including non-capitalist ones, have pursued imperial policies. "The acceptance of [Hobson's] theory," he states, was based on "the attractiveness of its economic reasoning and on the blatant truth that the advanced capitalist states of the day were, indeed, among history's most impressive builders of empire ... Then why not identify capitalism with Imperialism?"[11] Waltz answers his own question this way: "All kinds of states," including the non-capitalist Soviet Union,* "have pursued Imperialist policies."[12] Therefore, the economic explanation should not trump reasons of grand strategy.

Mearsheimer agrees, to a point, that America is pursuing an imperialist foreign policy, and that this threatens domestic freedoms by encouraging militarism* and a "security culture."[13] Mearsheimer and Hobson also agree on the domestic point.[14] They disagree, however, on the reasons behind this imperial project, with Mearsheimer writing that "the root cause of America's troubles is that it adopted a flawed grand strategy after the Cold War ... pursuing global dominance, or what might alternatively be called global hegemony."*[15]

If economic objectives are not behind this plan, then what is? For Mearsheimer, the answer is evident: "Making sure that the United States remains the most powerful state in the international system; and spreading democracy across the globe, in effect, making the world in America's image."[16] In essence, modern neorealism believes that America pursues power with security in mind first and foremost, and with economic motivations irrelevant.

So while critics of modern imperialism (such as Harvey and Meiksins Wood) see the 2003 invasion of Iraq as a rational pursuit of capitalist interests, Waltz and Mearsheimer see it only as a massive mistake.

---

1. Gregory Nowell, "Hobson's *Imperialism*: Its Historical Validity and Contemporary Relevance," in *The Political Economy of Imperialism: Critical Appraisals* (Lanham, MD: Rowman and Littlefield, 1999), 102.
2. Nowell, "Hobson's *Imperialism*," 104.
3. David Harvey, *The New Imperialism* (Oxford: Oxford University Press, 2005), 18.
4. Ellen Meiksins Wood, *Empire of Capital* (London: Verso, 2005), 144.
5. John Mearsheimer, *The Tragedy of Great Power Politics* (New York: W. W. Norton, 2001), 169.
6. Harvey, *New Imperialism*, 180.
7. Harvey, *New Imperialism*, 180.
8. John Hobson, *Imperialism: A Study* (Nottingham: Spokesman, 2011), 85.
9. Meiksins Wood, *Empire of Capital*, 130.
10. Ellen Meiksins Wood, "Logics of Power: A Conversation with David Harvey," *Historical Materialism* 14, no. 4 (2006): 13.
11. Kenneth Waltz, *Theory of International Politics* (Reading, MA: Addison Wesley, 1979), 25.
12. Waltz, *Theory*, 36.
13. John Mearsheimer, "Imperial by Design," *The National Interest* 111 (2011): 17.
14. Hobson, *Imperialism*, 142.
15. Mearsheimer, "Imperial by Design," 18.
16. Mearsheimer, "Imperial by Design," 19.

MODULE 12
WHERE NEXT?

KEY POINTS

- Hobson's work will remain relevant as long as states pursue aggressive foreign policies that can be linked to economic gains.
- *Imperialism* will continue to be part of a long-standing tradition that accuses the capitalist* system of being "rigged" in favor of one class or another — the French economist Thomas Piketty's* book *Capital in the Twenty-First Century* can be seen as continuing this project.
- *Imperialism* is seminal not for its core argument, but for uncovering the network of relationships — even now poorly understood — that drive the engine of capitalist expansion.

Potential

The Canadian scholar Michael Ignatieff* has insisted that America's "war on terror"* is a rhetorical cover for an imperial project: he considers American foreign policy imperial even though it does not overtly annex territory abroad. "What else can you call America's legions of soldiers, spooks, and Special Forces straddling the globe" than an imperial force?[1] You could call it a ruse of sorts. This post-Hobson perspective sees the "war on terror" as a means to justify foreign intervention rather than as a true representation of America's security interests.

Additionally, Hobson's concept of imperialism* requires that the imperial project be rational for private economic interests — at the expense of the public interest. In his *Farewell Address,* US

President Dwight D. Eisenhower* revealed this relationship between militarism, imperial expansion, and the price to the public. In fact, he memorably coined the phrase "military-industrial complex,"* warning: "In councils of government we must guard against the influence of the acquisition of unwarranted influence, sought or unsought, by the military-industrial complex."2

To allow this confluence of interests to control policy, according to Eisenhower, would decrease domestic liberty and increase militarism* abroad. Continuing anxiety over the complex is brought into the present day with an article published in the *Independent* newspaper in 2014, "Ike Was Right All Along," in which the British journalist Rupert Cornwell* writes: "The true tragedy is not quite the one that Eisenhower imagined. The US by itself accounts for roughly half of military spending worldwide. How much better if some of that money would be used to improve the country's education and infrastructure, or provide health care for all, or increase foreign aid, rather than protecting America from threats that geography alone renders illusory?"3

Hobson's assertion that militarism abroad would ultimately erode domestic liberty has made it into popular discourse. The American law scholar Jeffrey Rosen's* criticism of the USA PATRIOT Act* is an example. The acronym, which clearly invoked American patriotism,* stood for *Providing Appropriate Tools Required to Intercept and Obstruct Terrorism* — but it also cloaked the actions and dangers behind the law: "From the beginning, Democratic and Republican critics of the Patriot Act warned that its extraordinary surveillance powers would be used to investigate political dissent and low-level offences rather than terrorism. ... A 2007 report by the Inspector General of the Justice Department found 'widespread and serious abuse' of authority by the FBI [Federal Bureau of Investigation]* under the Patriot Act — even though these actions involved no clear connection to terrorism."[4]

> *"This conjunction of an immense military establishment and a large arms industry is new in the American experience. The total influence — economic, political, even spiritual — is felt in every city, every State house, every office of the Federal government."*
> —— Dwight D. Eisenhower, *Farewell Address*

Future Directions

One of the most exciting, ongoing aspects of the project Hobson initiated concerns economics.

The book by the French economist Thomas Piketty, *Capital in the Twenty-First Century* (2014), takes the premise that "there is no fundamental reason why we should believe that growth is automatically balanced," and that capitalist development leads to more inequality, rather than less.[5] Piketty's first major conclusion is that the distribution of wealth is not the result of "economic determinism" — there are no laws internal to the capitalist economic system that offer any guarantees about the distribution of wealth.[6]

Most importantly — in terms of pushing Hobson's idea

to its natural conclusion — Piketty argues that "the history of the distribution of wealth has always been deeply political."[7] Thus, Piketty and Hobson's theories hold common ground in terms of how disproportionate political weight can be given to the interests of the wealthy. In Hobson's case, that is how the wealthy induce politicians to pursue imperial policies that secure their capital investments abroad; in Piketty's case, that is how political decisions on the distribution of wealth favor the interests of the wealthy.

Piketty's book makes another key assertion: those at the very top of major companies can, and often do, collude to act in their own interests, contrary to those of the public — and this is much akin to Hobson's conspiracy theory but there are two important differences.

First, Piketty believes the collusion exists within the business world, rather than between business and government (as Hobson does). Secondly, Piketty's reasoning for this is clear, and not prone to slippage (as Hobson's is). That said, the two men argue that the nature of the collusion is actually very simple: "Top managers by and large have the power to set their own remuneration." They agree how much they are paid, in other words — and they happen to set that number very high indeed.[8]

In fact, a 2014 report by the American trade union* organization the American Federation of Labor and Congress of Industrial Organizations listed the pay of American chief executives at *331 times* that of the companies' employees — up from nearly 50 times in 1983.[9]

Summary

John Hobson's 1902 book *Imperialism: A Study* deserves special attention because it remains one of the most powerful and strident criticisms of imperial policy to come out of the tradition of British political radicalism.*

The work partly inspired Vladimir Lenin* to write his book *Capitalism is the Highest Stage of Imperialism*, and has served as a key inspiration for Marxist* thought from the twentieth century through to today. Even one of the book's harshest twentieth-century critics, the historian D. K. Fieldhouse,* credits *Imperialism* with a number of major achievements: Hobson demonstrated that imperialism was an irrational public policy, and encouraged "British, and subsequently world, opinion to accept his special definition of the word Imperialism."[10]

Hobson's "special" definition of imperialism involves more than just a military adventure beyond a nation's borders: it represents a capitalist project to open markets, exploit resources, and export capital. All of this, Hobson believed, amounts to a cynical enterprise that plays on public spiritedness to secure major gains for private investors — all at the expense of the public good both in the home country and in the colony.

While Hobson's analysis was largely discarded as conspiracy theory because it cast financiers* as larger-than-life power brokers over the state, it still boasts enough power to have taken on the status of a basic, foundational viewpoint. If anything, it is capitalism itself that has become larger than life — and thus for today's readers and thinkers, *Imperialism* holds value.

1. Michael Ignatieff, "Nation Building Lite," *New York Times*, July 28, 2002, accessed February 22, 2014, http://www.nytimes.com/2002/07/28/magazine/nation-building-lite.html.
2. Dwight D. Eisenhower, *Farewell Address*, accessed February 17, 2014, http://www.americanrhetoric.com/speeches/dwightdeisenhowerfarewell.html.
3. Rupert Cornwell, "Ike Was Right All Along: The Danger of the Military Industrial Complex," January 17, 2011, accessed February 22, 2014, http://www.independent.co.uk/news/world/americas/ike-was-right-all-along-the-danger-of-the-militaryindustrial-complex-2186133.html.
4. Jeffrey Rosen, "Too Much Power?," *International New York Times*, September 7, 2007, accessed February 22, 2014, http://www.nytimes.com/roomfordebate/2011/09/07/do-we-still-need-the-patriot-act/the-patriot-act-gives-too-much-power-to-law-enforcement.
5. Thomas Piketty, Anthony Atkinson, and Emmanuel Saez, *Capital in the Twenty-First Century* (Cambridge, MA: Belknap Press, 2014), 15.
6. Piketty et al., *Capital*, 20.
7. Piketty et al., *Capital*, 20.
8. Piketty et al., *Capital*, 24.
9. "PayWatch 2014," AFL-CIO report, accessed July 9, 2015, http://edit.aflcio.org/Corporate-Watch/Paywatch-2014.
10. D. K. Fieldhouse, "Imperialism: A Historiographical Revision," *Economic History Review* 14, no. 2 (1961): 187.

GLOSSARY OF TERMS

1. **Anti-Semitism:** discrimination or hatred directed toward Jewish people.

2. **Boer War (1899–1902):** a conflict between the British Empire and the Boer Republics (lands in present-day South Africa then claimed and governed by the descendants of Dutch settlers — the Boers). The end of the war saw the Empire annex the Boer territories at considerable military and civilian cost to both sides.

3. **Capitalism:** an economic system in which the means of production (generally resources and factories) are owned as private property, with the goal of selling products to make profit in a market economy.

4. **Classical liberalism:** the political belief that the liberty of the individual ought to be maximized by limitation of state power; it advocates private property and minimal intervention.

5. **Cold War (1947–91):** a period of tension between the United States and the Soviet Union and aligned nations. While the two blocs never engaged in direct military conflict, they engaged in covert and proxy wars (sponsored opposing sides in military conflicts), and espionage against one another.

6. **Colonialism:** as Hobson understands it, colonialism occurs when a developed nation reproduces itself on otherwise unused land, extending full rights of citizenship to all those who move there. Hobson sees this as the opposite of imperialism.

7. **Communism:** a political ideology that relies on the state ownership of the means of production, collectivization of labor, and abolition of social class. It was the ideology of the Soviet Union (1922–91), and contrasted with free market capitalism during the Cold War.

8. **Concentration camp:** a camp where non-military, perceived enemies of the state are detained in poor conditions and often without trial.

9. **Eurocentrism:** the idea that European cultural history provides some kind of "standard" against which all others are judged.

10. **Fabian Society:** an English socialist organization founded in 1884, seeking to influence the parliamentary process through long-term pressure.

11. **Federal Bureau of Investigation (FBI):** an American governmental institution

serving to investigate acts of espionage, terrorism, and major crime.

12. **Finance capitalism:** the aspect of a capitalist economy specifically concerned with finance (private investment made with the aim of private profit).

13. **Financier:** a person whose primary profession is investing in, owning, and lending large sums of money to business ventures.

14. **Globalization:** a number of processes of international integration (both planned and organic) that arise from a global interchange of ideas, culture, and material goods.

15. **Hegemony:** dominance in all forms over all others, especially by a state or military entity.

16. **Illiberal:** contrary to liberal political tenets: either unconcerned with promoting individual liberty or concerned with actively limiting individual liberty.

17. **Imperialism:** for Hobson, this is the forcible subjugation of one nationality in one territory by another for economic ends.

18. **Institutional economics:** the study of the role of previously existing institutions and ideas in shaping economic behavior.

19. **International Monetary Fund (IMF):** an international institution founded on the principle of promoting cooperation and good financial governance.

20. **Iraq War (2003–11):** an armed conflict initially fought between Iraq and the United States and its allies; once the initial military aims of the United States and its allies had been achieved, a protracted insurgency began. The justification for war was that Saddam Hussein, the leader of Iraq, was secretly building weapons of mass destruction. No such weapons were found.

21. **Jingoism:** aggressive patriotism.

22. **Leninist imperialism:** an understanding of imperialism expounded by the Russian revolutionary leader Vladimir Lenin that bears many similarities to that of Hobson. Lenin believed middle-class financiers exported capital to the developing world in order to exploit the poor. He differed from Hobson in concluding that this exploitation was to forestall revolution by the lower classes

in the home country, and that revolution was the only solution to both capitalism and imperialism.

23. **Liberal Party (1859–1988):** a political party of the United Kingdom. It favored welfare and advancing trade. In 1988, it merged with the Social Democratic party to create the still-active Liberal Democratic Party.

24. **Liberalism:** an approach to politics that favors individual liberty and the promotion of welfare.

25. **Marxism:** a broad school of social analysis that is characterized by materialism, class conflict, and determinism, founded on the work of the German political philosopher Karl Marx.

26. **Mercantilism:** the dominant economic policy of Western Europe until the nineteenth century. It aimed for a positive balance of trade (meaning that trade should be primarily internal), and therefore was a key driver of colonial expansion.

27. **Militarism:** the belief that the military is the most important element of a state, and that the use of force is an appropriate (and often necessary) element of foreign policy.

28. **Military-industrial complex:** the network of relationships between American lawmakers, military general staff, and the private arms industry.

29. **Nationalism:** extreme patriotism, often paired with disdain for other nations.

30. **Neorealism:** a school of international relations theory which assumes that structural constraints — anarchy and the distribution of world power — will determine actor behavior rather than human agency.

31. **New liberals:** followers of liberal thought who favored government intervention to ensure economic social justice.

32. **Oligarchy:** a state of affairs in which a small number of individuals share power over others.

33. **Oligopoly:** a state of affairs in which a small number of producers share a market.

34. **PATRIOT Act (2001):** a piece of American legislation that allows law enforcement agencies unprecedented powers of surveillance of American citizens. Also known as the USA PATRIOT Act.

35. **Patriotism:** having love and reverence for one's own country.

36. **Political economy:** a branch of the academic discipline of economics. "Political economy" usually refers to the study of the ways that political systems and institutions affect the running of national economies.

37. **Post-Marxism:** a school of thought that builds on standard Marxist thought by rejecting a number of its key assumptions. For example, post-Marxists do not believe that capitalists use the state as a tool, as did Marx; for them, the notion of a "state" is inherently "capitalist."

38. **Progressive taxation:** a system where the tax rate increases as the taxable amount increases; the resulting average tax rate is less than the highest marginal tax rate.

39. **Prototype:** the "first run" of some product or service (usually done as a "proof of concept").

40. **Radicalism (eighteenth to nineteenth century):** a left-wing British political movement rooted in demands for reform of the electoral system to widen the franchise. It eventually encompassed multiple intellectual movements to increase political liberalism.

41. **Say's Law:** named for the French economist Jean-Baptiste Say (1767–1832), Say's Law argues that production is the source of demand. In other words, when an individual produces, he will be paid, and then purchase the production of others, who will in turn purchase his, and so on.

42. **Scramble for Africa (1881–1914):** a period of energetic expansion by European powers into African territories to claim direct rule of colonies and exploit the continent's resources.

43. **Social Darwinism:** the use of scientific language and the use of (supposedly) scientific techniques to support racist beliefs. It was notably practiced in Germany by the Nazi Party in the 1930s and 1940s as part of a racist/anti-Semitic

| Glossary of Terms

political platform. The term has now taken on a pejorative meaning.

44. **Social liberalism:** the political belief that liberty (liberalism) ought to be managed by state organisms (socialism). Social liberals believe in a market economy as well as a redistributive program.

45. **Socialism:** the political belief that the factors of production of goods should be owned "socially" by the people, rather than by individual capitalists.

46. **Soviet Union:** a federation of communist states that existed between 1922 and 1991, centered primarily on Russia and its neighbors in Eastern Europe and the northern half of Asia. It was the communist pole of the Cold War, with the United States as its main "rival."

47. **Trade unionism:** the organization of laborers in a common profession who come together to bargain with purchasers of their labor, and also to influence policy.

48. **Underconsumption theory:** the theory that economies stagnate due to inadequate demand relative to supply. It was largely replaced in the 1930s by Keynesian theories — that is, theories derived from the ideas of the economist John Maynard Keynes — of aggregate demand.

49. **"War on terror":** a term commonly applied to American-led actions throughout the Middle East against non-state "terrorist" actors, including al Qaeda and ISIS. The drone campaign in Pakistan, the occupation of Afghanistan, and other covert and overt operations are rolled into this effort.

50. **World Bank:** an international financial institution established to manage economic aid and make loans to members, allowing them to overcome financial crises.

51. **World War I:** also called the Great War, World War I was fought between 1914 and 1918. During the war, the Allied forces (led by France, Italy, Russia, the United Kingdom and the United States) and the Central powers (led by Austria-Hungary, Bulgaria, Germany, and the Ottoman Empire) fought, leaving 16 million people dead.

PEOPLE MENTIONED IN THE TEXT

1. **Norman Angell (1872–1967)** was an English lecturer and author, and a prominent member of the idealist school of international relations.
2. **Hannah Arendt (1906–75)** was a German political thinker. Her work deals with the nature of power and control.
3. **Michael Barratt Brown (1918–2015)** was a British political economist and Marxist scholar. He was particularly concerned with foreign policy.
4. **Jeremy Bentham (1748–1832)** was a British philosopher and liberal social reformer. He is considered the founding figure of the philosophy of utilitarianism (according to which, roughly, an action can be judged "good" if it serves to make people happy).
5. **George W. Bush (b. 1946)** is an American politician. He was the 43rd president of the United States, from 2001 to 2009. The attacks of September 11, 2001, the invasion of Iraq in 2003, and the ongoing occupation of Afghanistan occurred under his presidency.
6. **P. J. Cain (b. 1941)** is a British professor of history at Sheffield University. He specializes in the history of English liberal thought.
7. **Joseph Chamberlain (1836–1914)** was a British politician who served as secretary of state for the colonies, presiding over the Second Boer War.
8. **Richard Cobden (1804–65)** was a British businessman and Liberal statesman, and an advocate of a liberal conception of international politics.
9. **Jeremy Corbyn (b. 1949)** is a British member of parliament and leader of the Labour Party from September 2015.
10. **Rupert Cornwell** is a British journalist, notable as the chief US correspondent of London's *Independent*.
11. **Dwight D. Eisenhower (1890–1969)** was an American politician and general, and president of the United States (1953–61).
12. **David Kenneth (D. K.) Fieldhouse (b. 1925)** is a historian of the British Empire at Jesus College, Cambridge.
13. **Thomas Hill Green (1836–82)** was an English liberal philosopher. He is well

known for the distinction he drew between negative liberty (the freedom of no restriction) and positive liberty (the freedom of being enabled).

14. **Michael Hardt (b. 1960)** is an American literary theorist and political philosopher.

15. **David Harvey (b. 1935)** is a British professor of geography specializing in social theory at the City University of NewYork. He is widely credited as one of the foremost Marxist critics of global capitalism.

16. **Michael Ignatieff (b. 1947)** is a Canadian academic specializing in international development, and is a former Liberal politician.

17. **Baron John Maynard Keynes (1883–1946)** was a British economist. He is widely referred to as the founder of modern macroeconomics for showing that perfectly free markets do not provide full employment.

18. **Vladimir Lenin (1870–1924)** was a Russian communist revolutionary politician. He was the first premier of the Soviet Union.

19. **John Locke (1632–1704)** was an English philosopher famous as one of the founders of classical liberalism, in which the freedom of the individual is emphasized and the power of the government is limited. He was a major thinker in the social contract school. His work *The Second Treatise on Government* is still widely considered groundbreaking.

20. **David Long** is a Canadian professor of international relations at Carleton University.

21. **John Lonsdale** is a historian and fellow of Trinity College, Cambridge specializing in African studies.

22. **Rosa Luxemburg (1871–1919)** was a Polish German Marxist thinker and founder of the predecessor to the Communist Party of Germany.

23. **Lars Magnusson (b. 1952)** is an economic historian at the University of Uppsala in Sweden. He is a key figure in the revival of Hobson scholarship.

24. **Karl Marx (1818–83)** was a German political philosopher famous for writing, among other works, *Capital* and *The Communist Manifesto*. His main idea, that

human society progresses from one stage to the next through class struggle, sits at the core of Marxism.

25. **John Mearsheimer (b. 1947)** is an American international relations professor and neorealist. He is the pioneer of "offensive realism," a contemporary reformulation of neorealism.

26. **Nathaniel Mehr** is a British journalist, author, and left-wing public intellectual.

27. **Ellen Meiksins Wood (b. 1942)** is an American Marxist historian and scholar, formerly of York University in Canada.

28. **John Stuart Mill (1806–73)** was an English liberal philosopher and political economist. He was a key early proponent of the right of the citizen to live free from state interference.

29. **Albert Mummery (1855–95)** was a British businessman and mountaineer.

30. **Antonio Negri (b. 1933)** is an Italian Marxist philosopher and political agitator. After living in exile in France, where he taught at the Sorbonne, he returned to Italy in 1997 to serve a 13-year prison sentence (commuted from 30 years) for alleged anti-state activity.

31. **Gregory Nowell** is an American professor of political economy specializing in Marxism and the international oil industry at the State University of NewYork.

32. **Thomas Piketty (b. 1971)** is a French economist and best-selling author (best known for *Capital in the Twenty-First Century*). His book argues that in the long run, income generated from capital outstrips that generated from individual worker wages.

33. **Cecil Rhodes (1853–1902)** was a British tycoon and politician in South Africa. He established the diamond company De Beers, which today accounts for 40 percent of the world's diamond trade.

34. **Jeffrey Rosen (b. 1964)** is an American legal academic at Yale Law School.

35. **John Ruskin (1819–1900)** was a British art critic, social thinker, and philanthropist. His famous book *Unto This Last* (1860) argued for a social element of economic thought.

36. **Jean-Baptiste Say (1767–1832)** was a French economist and businessman who developed Say's Law, according to which production is the source of demand. It is a principle of classical economics (a theoretical approach to economics opposed to government interference in the economy).

37. **Joseph Schumpeter (1883–1950)** was an Austrian economist and political thinker who wrote on many areas; some of his most famous work is on innovation and business. He believed economies were driven forward through invention and "creative destruction" (horses and buggies, for example, were replaced by trains).

38. **Adam Smith (1723–90)** was a Scottish political philosopher widely considered to be the founding father of economics as an academic discipline with his book *The Wealth of Nations* (1776).

39. **Thorstein Veblen (1857–1929)** was an American economist, sociologist, and founding thinker of institutional economics, a school of thought that suggested that capitalism was inefficient due to its inbuilt holdovers (institutions) from the past.

40. **Kenneth Waltz (1924–2013)** was an American international relations professor best known for reformulating realism in order to make it more scientific (often called neorealism).

WORKS CITED

1. Arendt, Hannah. *The Origins of Totalitarianism*. New York: Harcourt, 1968.
2. Arestis, Philip, and Malcolm Sawyer. *The Elgar Companion to Radical Political Economy*. Aldershot: Edward Elgar, 1994.
3. Auld, John. "The Liberal Pro-Boers." *Journal of British Studies* 14, no. 2 (1975): 78–101.
4. Barratt Brown, Michael. *After Imperialism*. London: Merlin, 1970.
5. ———. *The Economics of Imperialism*. London: Penguin, 1974.
6. Cain, P. J. *Hobson and Imperialism: Radicalism, New Liberalism, and Finance: 1887–1938*. Oxford: Oxford University Press, 2002.
7. ———. "Radicalism, Gladstone and the Liberal Critique of Disraelian 'Imperialism.'" In *Victorian Visions of Global Order: Empire and International Relations in Nineteenth-Century Political Thought*, edited by Duncan Bell, 215–38. Cambridge: Cambridge University Press, 2007.
8. Cornwell, Rupert. "Ike Was Right All Along: The Danger of the Military Industrial Complex," January 17, 2011. Accessed February 22, 2014. http://www.independent.co.uk/news/world/americas/ike-was-right-all-along-the-danger-of-the-militaryindustrial-complex-2186133.html.
9. Cunningham Wood, John D., and Wood, Robert D. *John A. Hobson: Critical Assessments of Leading Economists*. London: Routledge, 2003.
10. Edgell, Stephen, and Jules Townshend. "John Hobson, Thorstein Veblen, and the Phenomenon of Imperialism: Finance Capital, Patriotism, and War." *American Journal of Economics and Sociology* 51, no. 4 (1992): 401–20.
11. Eisenhower, Dwight D. *Farewell Address*. Accessed February 17, 2014. http://www.americanrhetoric.com/speeches/dwightdeisenhowerfarewell.html.
12. Fieldhouse, D. K. "Imperialism: An Historiographical Revision." *Economic History Review* 14, no. 2 (1961): 187–209.
13. Freeden, Michael. *Reappraising J. A. Hobson*. London: Unwin Hyman, 1990.
14. Green, T. H. "Liberal Legislation and Freedom of Contract." In *The Political Theory of T. H. Green: Selected Writings*, edited by John R. Rodman, 43–73.

New York: Meredith, 1964.
15. Hardt, Michael, and Antonio Negri. *Empire*. Cambridge, MA: Harvard University Press, 2000.
16. Harvey, David. *The New Imperialism*. Oxford: Oxford University Press, 2005.
17. Hobson, John. *Confessions of an Economic Heretic*. Hassocks: Harvester Press, 1976.*The Evolution of Modern Capitalism*. London: The Walter Scott Publishing Company, 1906.
18. ———. *Imperialism: A Study*. Nottingham: Spokesman, 2011.
19. ———. *The War in South Africa: Its Causes and Effects*. London: James Nisbet and Co. Ltd, 1900.
20. Ignatieff, Michael. "Nation Building Lite." *New York Times*, July 28, 2002. Accessed February 22, 2014. http://www.nytimes.com/2002/07/28/magazine/nation-building-lite.html.
21. Jahn, Beate. "Kant, Mill, and Illiberal Legacies in International Affairs." *International Organization* 59, no. 1 (2005): 177–207.
22. Keynes, John Maynard. "Review of *Gold, Prices, and Wages*." *Economic Journal* 23 (1913): 393.
23. Lenin, Vladimir. *Imperialism: The Highest Stage of Capitalism*. New York: International Publishers, 1939.
24. Locke, John. *Second Treatise of Government*. Edited by C. B. Macpherson. Indianapolis, IN: Hackett, 1980.
25. Long, David. "Paternalism and the Internationalization of Imperialism: J. A. Hobson on the International Government of the 'Lower Races.'" In *Imperialism and Internationalism in the Discipline of International Relations*, edited by David Long and Brian Schmidt, 71–93. Albany, NY: University of New York Press, 2005.
26. Lonsdale, John. "The European Scramble and Conquest in African History." In *The Cambridge History of Africa*. Vol. 6, c. 1870–c. 1905, edited by Roland Oliver and G. N. Sanderson, 680–766. Cambridge: Cambridge University Press, 1985.

27. Luxemburg, Rosa. *The Accumulation of Capital.* Accessed February 22, 2014. http://www.marxists.org/archive/luxemburg/1913/accumulation-capital/ch31.htm.

28. Magnusson, Lars. "Hobson and Imperialism: An Appraisal." In *J. A. Hobson after Fifty Years,* edited by John Pheby, 143–62. London: Macmillan, 1994.

29. Mearsheimer, John. "Imperial by Design." *The National Interest* 111 (2011): 16–34.

30. ———. *The Tragedy of Great Power Politics.* New York: W. W. Norton, 2001.

31. Meiksins Wood, Ellen. *Empire of Capital.* London: Verso, 2005.

32. ———. "Logics of Power: A Conversation with David Harvey." *Historical Materialism* 14, no. 4 (2006): 9–34.

33. Mill, John Stuart. *Principles of Political Economy with Some of Their Applications to Social Philosophy.* London: Longmans, 1865.

34. Mitchell, Harvey. "Hobson Revisited." *Journal of the History of Ideas* 26, no. 3 (1965): 397–416.

35. Morgan, Kenneth. "The Boer War and the Media." *Twentieth Century British History* 13, no. 1 (2002): 1–16.

36. Mummery, Albert, and John Hobson. *The Physiology of Industry; Being an Exposure of Certain Fallacies in Existing Theories of Economics.* London: John Murray, 1889.

37. Nowell, Gregory. "Hobson's *Imperialism*: Its Historical Validity and Contemporary Relevance." In *The Political Economy of Imperialism: Critical Appraisals,* edited by Ronald H. Chilcote, 85–109. Lanham, MD: Rowman and Littlefield, 1999.

38. Oliver, Roland, and Atmore, Anthony. *Africa since 1800.* Cambridge: Cambridge University Press, 2005.

39. Piketty, Thomas, Anthony Atkinson, and Emmanuel Saez. *Capital in the Twenty-First Century.* Cambridge, MA: Belknap Press, 2014.

40. Porter, Bernard. *Critics of Empire: British Radicals and the Imperial Challenge.*

London: I. B. Tauris, 2007.

41. Robertson, J. M. *Patriotism and Empire*. London: Grant Richards, 1900.

42. Rosen, Jeffrey. "Too Much Power?" *International New York Times*, September 7, 2007. Accessed February 22, 2014. http://www.nytimes.com/roomfordebate/2011/09/07/do-we-still-need-the-patriot-act/the-patriot-act-gives-too-much-power-to-law-enforcement.

43. Särkkä, Timo. *Hobson's Imperialism: A Study in Late Victorian Political Thought*. Jyväskylä: University of Jyväskylä, 2009.

44. Schneider, Michael. *J. A. Hobson*. London: Macmillan, 1996.

45. Schumpeter, Joseph. *Imperialism and Social Classes: Two Essays*. Translated by Heinz Norden. New York: Meridian, 2007.

46. Smith, Adam. *An Inquiry into the Nature and Causes of the Wealth of Nations*. London: Digireads, 2009.

47. Sullivan, Eileen. "Liberalism and Imperialism: J. S. Mill's Defence of the British Empire." *Journal of the History of Ideas* 44, no. 4 (1983): 599–617.

48. Veblen, Thorstein. *Absentee Ownership and Business Enterprise in Recent Times*. New York: Kelley, 1964.

49. Waltz, Kenneth. *Theory of International Politics*. Reading, MA: Addison Wesley, 1979.

原书作者简介

约翰·A.霍布森是一位政治经济学家，于 1858 年出生在英国德比郡的一个中产阶级家庭。他的父亲是一家报社的老板，他也最终成为一名记者。霍布森曾担任《曼彻斯特卫报》驻南非特派记者，对 19 世纪末爆发的第二次布尔战争进行过专题报道。正因为此，他逐渐形成了自己的激进主义理论，关注资本主义如何驱使一个国家建立帝国。霍布森于 1940 年逝世，在他去世前两年，其自传《一个异端经济学家的自白》得以出版。

本书作者简介

赖利·奎恩，获伦敦政治经济学院和牛津大学政治与国际关系专业硕士学位。

世界名著中的批判性思维

《世界思想宝库钥匙丛书》致力于深入浅出地阐释全世界著名思想家的观点，不论是谁、在何处都能了解到，从而推进批判性思维发展。

《世界思想宝库钥匙丛书》与世界顶尖大学的一流学者合作，为一系列学科中最有影响的著作推出新的分析文本，介绍其观点和影响。在这一不断扩展的系列中，每种选入的著作都代表了历经时间考验的思想典范。通过为这些著作提供必要背景、揭示原作者的学术渊源以及说明这些著作所产生的影响，本系列图书希望让读者以新视角看待这些划时代的经典之作。读者应学会思考、运用并挑战这些著作中的观点，而不是简单接受它们。

ABOUT THE AUTHOR OF THE ORIGINAL WORK

The political economist **John A. Hobson** was born in 1858 to a middle class family in Derbyshire, England. His father was a newspaper owner, and Hobson eventually became a journalist himself. As South Africa correspondent for the *Manchester Guardian*, he covered the Second Boer War at the very end of the nineteenth century. It was here that he began to develop his radical theories about how capitalism drove a nation's desire for empire building. Hobson died in 1940, two years after publishing his autobiography *Confessions of an Economic Heretic*.

ABOUT THE AUTHOR OF THE ANALYSIS

Riley Quinn holds master's degrees in politics and international relations from both LSE and the University of Oxford.

ABOUT MACAT
GREAT WORKS FOR CRITICAL THINKING

Macat is focused on making the ideas of the world's great thinkers accessible and comprehensible to everybody, everywhere, in ways that promote the development of enhanced critical thinking skills.

It works with leading academics from the world's top universities to produce new analyses that focus on the ideas and the impact of the most influential works ever written across a wide variety of academic disciplines. Each of the works that sit at the heart of its growing library is an enduring example of great thinking. But by setting them in context — and looking at the influences that shaped their authors, as well as the responses they provoked — Macat encourages readers to look at these classics and game-changers with fresh eyes. Readers learn to think, engage and challenge their ideas, rather than simply accepting them.

批判性思维与《帝国主义》

首要批判性思维技巧：分析

次要批判性思维技巧：评估

英国经济学家约翰·A.霍布森的《帝国主义》（1902）是帝国主义政治学与经济学研究领域的一部具有划时代意义的著作，该书从根本上动摇了帝国主义的基本信条。当时大英帝国统治着全球大部分地区，而作为一名坚定的自由主义者，霍布森对帝国主义思想的目标和主张深表怀疑。为了对他所认为的帝国主义的错误逻辑及不道德的政治观点进行批判，霍布森在该书中运用了一种犀利的分析方法来剖析帝国主义概念。他的主要洞见之一就是对帝国主义根源的不同观点进行评估；在这个过程中，他发现"帝国主义在本质上是一种民族主义"的普遍观点实际上是站不住脚的。相反，他通过仔细分析民族主义背后的间接及隐藏原因，证明了帝国主义在本质上是资本主义的产物。在他的分析中，我们可以清楚地看到，与其说帝国主义是一种政治意识形态，还不如说是出于开拓新市场和解决经济停滞问题的需要。霍布森的这部论著在当时颇具争议，它向我们展示了分析与评估在解构最广为接受的观点方面所具有的强大力量。

CRITICAL THINKING AND *IMPERIALISM*

- Primary critical thinking skill: ANALYSIS
- Secondary critical thinking skill: EVALUATION

English economist John Hobson's 1902 *Imperialism: A Study* was an epoch-making study of the politics and economics of imperialism that shook imperialist beliefs to their core. A committed liberal, Hobson was deeply sceptical about the aims and claims of imperialistic thought at a time when Britain's empire held sway over a vast portion of the globe. In order to critique what he saw as a falsely reasoned and immoral political view, Hobson's book took a cuttingly analytical approach to the idea of imperialism. One of his key insights was to evaluate arguments surrounding the origins of imperialism — a process in which he found the widely accepted claims that imperialism was essentially a question of nationalism to be, in fact, quite weak. Instead, his close analysis of the implicit and hidden reasons behind nationalism demonstrated that, at root, it was a product of capitalism. In his analysis, it becomes clear that less than a political ideology, imperialism stems from the need to open up new markets, and remedy economic stagnation. Deeply provocative at the time, Hobson's book shows just how powerful analysis and evaluation can be at deconstructing the most widely accepted of ideas.

《世界思想宝库钥匙丛书》简介

《世界思想宝库钥匙丛书》致力于为一系列在各领域产生重大影响的人文社科类经典著作提供独特的学术探讨。每一本读物都不仅仅是原经典著作的内容摘要，而是介绍并深入研究原经典著作的学术渊源、主要观点和历史影响。这一丛书的目的是提供一套学习资料，以促进读者掌握批判性思维，从而更全面、深刻地去理解重要思想。

每一本读物分为3个部分：学术渊源、学术思想和学术影响，每个部分下有4个小节。这些章节旨在从各个方面研究原经典著作及其反响。

由于独特的体例，每一本读物不但易于阅读，而且另有一项优点：所有读物的编排体例相同，读者在进行某个知识层面的调查或研究时可交叉参阅多本该丛书中的相关读物，从而开启跨领域研究的路径。

为了方便阅读，每本读物最后还列出了术语表和人名表（在书中则以星号＊标记），此外还有参考文献。

《世界思想宝库钥匙丛书》与剑桥大学合作，理清了批判性思维的要点，即如何通过6种技能来进行有效思考。其中3种技能让我们能够理解问题，另3种技能让我们有能力解决问题。这6种技能合称为"批判性思维PACIER模式"，它们是：

分析：了解如何建立一个观点；
评估：研究一个观点的优点和缺点；
阐释：对意义所产生的问题加以理解；
创造性思维：提出新的见解，发现新的联系；
解决问题：提出切实有效的解决办法；
理性化思维：创建有说服力的观点。

THE MACAT LIBRARY

The Macat Library is a series of unique academic explorations of seminal works in the humanities and social sciences — books and papers that have had a significant and widely recognised impact on their disciplines. It has been created to serve as much more than just a summary of what lies between the covers of a great book. It illuminates and explores the influences on, ideas of, and impact of that book. Our goal is to offer a learning resource that encourages critical thinking and fosters a better, deeper understanding of important ideas.

Each publication is divided into three Sections: Influences, Ideas, and Impact. Each Section has four Modules. These explore every important facet of the work, and the responses to it.

This Section-Module structure makes a Macat Library book easy to use, but it has another important feature. Because each Macat book is written to the same format, it is possible (and encouraged!) to cross-reference multiple Macat books along the same lines of inquiry or research. This allows the reader to open up interesting interdisciplinary pathways.

To further aid your reading, lists of glossary terms and people mentioned are included at the end of this book (these are indicated by an asterisk [*] throughout) — as well as a list of works cited.

Macat has worked with the University of Cambridge to identify the elements of critical thinking and understand the ways in which six different skills combine to enable effective thinking.

Three allow us to fully understand a problem; three more give us the tools to solve it. Together, these six skills make up the PACIER model of critical thinking. They are:

ANALYSIS — understanding how an argument is built
EVALUATION — exploring the strengths and weaknesses of an argument
INTERPRETATION — understanding issues of meaning
CREATIVE THINKING — coming up with new ideas and fresh connections
PROBLEM-SOLVING — producing strong solutions
REASONING — creating strong arguments

"《世界思想宝库钥匙丛书》提供了独一无二的跨学科学习和研究工具。它介绍那些革新了各自学科研究的经典著作，还邀请全世界一流专家和教育机构进行严谨的分析，为每位读者打开世界顶级教育的大门。"

—— 安德烈亚斯·施莱歇尔，
经济合作与发展组织教育与技能司司长

"《世界思想宝库钥匙丛书》直面大学教育的巨大挑战……他们组建了一支精干而活跃的学者队伍，来推出在研究广度上颇具新意的教学材料。"

—— 布罗尔斯教授、勋爵，剑桥大学前校长

"《世界思想宝库钥匙丛书》的愿景令人赞叹。它通过分析和阐释那些曾深刻影响人类思想以及社会、经济发展的经典文本，提供了新的学习方法。它推动批判性思维，这对于任何社会和经济体来说都是至关重要的。这就是未来的学习方法。"

—— 查尔斯·克拉克阁下，英国前教育大臣

"对于那些影响了各自领域的著作，《世界思想宝库钥匙丛书》能让人们立即了解到围绕那些著作展开的评论性言论，这让该系列图书成为在这些领域从事研究的师生们不可或缺的资源。"

—— 威廉·特朗佐教授，加利福尼亚大学圣地亚哥分校

"Macat offers an amazing first-of-its-kind tool for interdisciplinary learning and research. Its focus on works that transformed their disciplines and its rigorous approach, drawing on the world's leading experts and educational institutions, opens up a world-class education to anyone."

—— Andreas Schleicher, Director for Education and Skills, Organisation for Economic Co-operation and Development

"Macat is taking on some of the major challenges in university education... They have drawn together a strong team of active academics who are producing teaching materials that are novel in the breadth of their approach."

—— Prof Lord Broers, former Vice-Chancellor of the University of Cambridge

"The Macat vision is exceptionally exciting. It focuses upon new modes of learning which analyse and explain seminal texts which have profoundly influenced world thinking and so social and economic development. It promotes the kind of critical thinking which is essential for any society and economy. This is the learning of the future."

—— Rt Hon Charles Clarke, former UK Secretary of State for Education

"The Macat analyses provide immediate access to the critical conversation surrounding the books that have shaped their respective discipline, which will make them an invaluable resource to all of those, students and teachers, working in the field."

—— Prof William Tronzo, University of California at San Diego

The Macat Library
世界思想宝库钥匙丛书

TITLE	中文书名	类别
An Analysis of Arjun Appadurai's *Modernity at Large: Cultural Dimensions of Globalization*	解析阿尔君·阿帕杜莱《消失的现代性：全球化的文化维度》	人类学
An Analysis of Claude Lévi-Strauss's *Structural Anthropology*	解析克劳德·列维-斯特劳斯《结构人类学》	人类学
An Analysis of Marcel Mauss's *The Gift*	解析马塞尔·莫斯《礼物》	人类学
An Analysis of Jared M. Diamond's *Guns, Germs, and Steel: The Fate of Human Societies*	解析贾雷德·M. 戴蒙德《枪炮、病菌与钢铁：人类社会的命运》	人类学
An Analysis of Clifford Geertz's *The Interpretation of Cultures*	解析克利福德·格尔茨《文化的解释》	人类学
An Analysis of Philippe Ariès's *Centuries of Childhood: A Social History of Family Life*	解析菲力浦·阿利埃斯《儿童的世纪：旧制度下的儿童和家庭生活》	人类学
An Analysis of W. Chan Kim & Renée Mauborgne's *Blue Ocean Strategy*	解析金伟灿/勒妮·莫博涅《蓝海战略》	商业
An Analysis of John P. Kotter's *Leading Change*	解析约翰·P. 科特《领导变革》	商业
An Analysis of Michael E. Porter's *Competitive Strategy: Techniques for Analyzing Industries and Competitors*	解析迈克尔·E. 波特《竞争战略：分析产业和竞争对手的技术》	商业
An Analysis of Jean Lave & Etienne Wenger's *Situated Learning: Legitimate Peripheral Participation*	解析琼·莱夫/艾蒂纳·温格《情境学习：合法的边缘性参与》	商业
An Analysis of Douglas McGregor's *The Human Side of Enterprise*	解析道格拉斯·麦格雷戈《企业的人性面》	商业
An Analysis of Milton Friedman's *Capitalism and Freedom*	解析米尔顿·弗里德曼《资本主义与自由》	商业
An Analysis of Ludwig von Mises's *The Theory of Money and Credit*	解析路德维希·冯·米塞斯《货币和信用理论》	经济学
An Analysis of Adam Smith's *The Wealth of Nations*	解析亚当·斯密《国富论》	经济学
An Analysis of Thomas Piketty's *Capital in the Twenty-First Century*	解析托马斯·皮凯蒂《21世纪资本论》	经济学
An Analysis of Nassim Nicholas Taleb's *The Black Swan: The Impact of the Highly Improbable*	解析纳西姆·尼古拉斯·塔勒布《黑天鹅：如何应对不可预知的未来》	经济学
An Analysis of Ha-Joon Chang's *Kicking Away the Ladder*	解析张夏准《富国陷阱：发达国家为何踢开梯子》	经济学
An Analysis of Thomas Robert Malthus's *An Essay on the Principle of Population*	解析托马斯·罗伯特·马尔萨斯《人口论》	经济学

An Analysis of John Maynard Keynes's *The General Theory of Employment, Interest and Money*	解析约翰·梅纳德·凯恩斯《就业、利息和货币通论》	经济学
An Analysis of Milton Friedman's *The Role of Monetary Policy*	解析米尔顿·弗里德曼《货币政策的作用》	经济学
An Analysis of Burton G. Malkiel's *A Random Walk Down Wall Street*	解析伯顿·G.马尔基尔《漫步华尔街》	经济学
An Analysis of Friedrich A. Hayek's *The Road to Serfdom*	解析弗里德里希·A.哈耶克《通往奴役之路》	经济学
An Analysis of Charles P. Kindleberger's *Manias, Panics, and Crashes: A History of Financial Crises*	解析查尔斯·P.金德尔伯格《疯狂、惊恐和崩溃：金融危机史》	经济学
An Analysis of Amartya Sen's *Development as Freedom*	解析阿马蒂亚·森《以自由看待发展》	经济学
An Analysis of Rachel Carson's *Silent Spring*	解析蕾切尔·卡森《寂静的春天》	地理学
An Analysis of Charles Darwin's *On the Origin of Species: by Means of Natural Selection, or The Preservation of Favoured Races in the Struggle for Life*	解析查尔斯·达尔文《物种起源》	地理学
An Analysis of World Commission on Environment and Development's *The Brundtland Report: Our Common Future*	解析世界环境与发展委员会《布伦特兰报告：我们共同的未来》	地理学
An Analysis of James E. Lovelock's *Gaia: A New Look at Life on Earth*	解析詹姆斯·E.拉伍洛克《盖娅：地球生命的新视野》	地理学
An Analysis of Paul Kennedy's *The Rise and Fall of the Great Powers: Economic Change and Military Conflict from 1500–2000*	解析保罗·肯尼迪《大国的兴衰：1500—2000年的经济变革与军事冲突》	历史
An Analysis of Janet L. Abu-Lughod's *Before European Hegemony: The World System A. D. 1250–1350*	解析珍妮特·L.阿布-卢格霍德《欧洲霸权之前：1250—1350年的世界体系》	历史
An Analysis of Alfred W. Crosby's *The Columbian Exchange: Biological and Cultural Consequences of 1492*	解析艾尔弗雷德·W.克罗斯比《哥伦布大交换：1492年以后的生物影响和文化冲击》	历史
An Analysis of Tony Judt's *Postwar: A History of Europe since 1945*	解析托尼·朱特《战后欧洲史》	历史
An Analysis of Richard J. Evans's *In Defence of History*	解析理查德·J.艾文斯《捍卫历史》	历史
An Analysis of Eric Hobsbawm's *The Age of Revolution: Europe 1789–1848*	解析艾瑞克·霍布斯鲍姆《革命的年代：欧洲1789—1848年》	历史

An Analysis of Roland Barthes's *Mythologies*	解析罗兰·巴特《神话学》	文学与批判理论
An Analysis of Simone de Beauvoir's *The Second Sex*	解析西蒙娜·德·波伏娃《第二性》	文学与批判理论
An Analysis of Edward W. Said's *Orientalism*	解析爱德华·W. 萨义德《东方主义》	文学与批判理论
An Analysis of Virginia Woolf's *A Room of One's Own*	解析弗吉尼亚·伍尔芙《一间自己的房间》	文学与批判理论
An Analysis of Judith Butler's *Gender Trouble*	解析朱迪斯·巴特勒《性别麻烦》	文学与批判理论
An Analysis of Ferdinand de Saussure's *Course in General Linguistics*	解析费尔迪南·德·索绪尔《普通语言学教程》	文学与批判理论
An Analysis of Susan Sontag's *On Photography*	解析苏珊·桑塔格《论摄影》	文学与批判理论
An Analysis of Walter Benjamin's *The Work of Art in the Age of Mechanical Reproduction*	解析瓦尔特·本雅明《机械复制时代的艺术作品》	文学与批判理论
An Analysis of W. E. B. Du Bois's *The Souls of Black Folk*	解析W.E.B. 杜波依斯《黑人的灵魂》	文学与批判理论
An Analysis of Plato's *The Republic*	解析柏拉图《理想国》	哲学
An Analysis of Plato's *Symposium*	解析柏拉图《会饮篇》	哲学
An Analysis of Aristotle's *Metaphysics*	解析亚里士多德《形而上学》	哲学
An Analysis of Aristotle's *Nicomachean Ethics*	解析亚里士多德《尼各马可伦理学》	哲学
An Analysis of Immanuel Kant's *Critique of Pure Reason*	解析伊曼努尔·康德《纯粹理性批判》	哲学
An Analysis of Ludwig Wittgenstein's *Philosophical Investigations*	解析路德维希·维特根斯坦《哲学研究》	哲学
An Analysis of G. W. F. Hegel's *Phenomenology of Spirit*	解析G. W. F. 黑格尔《精神现象学》	哲学
An Analysis of Baruch Spinoza's *Ethics*	解析巴鲁赫·斯宾诺莎《伦理学》	哲学
An Analysis of Hannah Arendt's *The Human Condition*	解析汉娜·阿伦特《人的境况》	哲学
An Analysis of G. E. M. Anscombe's *Modern Moral Philosophy*	解析G. E. M. 安斯康姆《现代道德哲学》	哲学
An Analysis of David Hume's *An Enquiry Concerning Human Understanding*	解析大卫·休谟《人类理解研究》	哲学

An Analysis of Søren Kierkegaard's *Fear and Trembling*	解析索伦·克尔凯郭尔《恐惧与战栗》	哲学
An Analysis of René Descartes's *Meditations on First Philosophy*	解析勒内·笛卡尔《第一哲学沉思录》	哲学
An Analysis of Friedrich Nietzsche's *On the Genealogy of Morality*	解析弗里德里希·尼采《论道德的谱系》	哲学
An Analysis of Gilbert Ryle's *The Concept of Mind*	解析吉尔伯特·赖尔《心的概念》	哲学
An Analysis of Thomas Kuhn's *The Structure of Scientific Revolutions*	解析托马斯·库恩《科学革命的结构》	哲学
An Analysis of John Stuart Mill's *Utilitarianism*	解析约翰·斯图亚特·穆勒《功利主义》	哲学
An Analysis of Aristotle's *Politics*	解析亚里士多德《政治学》	政治学
An Analysis of Niccolò Machiavelli's *The Prince*	解析尼科洛·马基雅维利《君主论》	政治学
An Analysis of Karl Marx's *Capital*	解析卡尔·马克思《资本论》	政治学
An Analysis of Benedict Anderson's *Imagined Communities*	解析本尼迪克特·安德森《想象的共同体》	政治学
An Analysis of Samuel P. Huntington's *The Clash of Civilizations and the Remaking of World Order*	解析塞缪尔·P.亨廷顿《文明的冲突与世界秩序的重建》	政治学
An Analysis of Alexis de Tocqueville's *Democracy in America*	解析阿列克西·德·托克维尔《论美国的民主》	政治学
An Analysis of John A. Hobson's *Imperialism: A Study*	解析约翰·A.霍布森《帝国主义》	政治学
An Analysis of Thomas Paine's *Common Sense*	解析托马斯·潘恩《常识》	政治学
An Analysis of John Rawls's *A Theory of Justice*	解析约翰·罗尔斯《正义论》	政治学
An Analysis of Francis Fukuyama's *The End of History and the Last Man*	解析弗朗西斯·福山《历史的终结与最后的人》	政治学
An Analysis of John Locke's *Two Treatises of Government*	解析约翰·洛克《政府论》	政治学
An Analysis of Sun Tzu's *The Art of War*	解析孙武《孙子兵法》	政治学
An Analysis of Henry Kissinger's *World Order: Reflections on the Character of Nations and the Course of History*	解析亨利·基辛格《世界秩序》	政治学
An Analysis of Jean-Jacques Rousseau's *The Social Contract*	解析让-雅克·卢梭《社会契约论》	政治学

An Analysis of Odd Arne Westad's *The Global Cold War: Third World Interventions and the Making of Our Times*	解析文安立《全球冷战：美苏对第三世界的干涉与当代世界的形成》	政治学
An Analysis of Sigmund Freud's *The Interpretation of Dreams*	解析西格蒙德·弗洛伊德《梦的解析》	心理学
An Analysis of William James' *The Principles of Psychology*	解析威廉·詹姆斯《心理学原理》	心理学
An Analysis of Philip Zimbardo's *The Lucifer Effect*	解析菲利普·津巴多《路西法效应》	心理学
An Analysis of Leon Festinger's *A Theory of Cognitive Dissonance*	解析利昂·费斯汀格《认知失调论》	心理学
An Analysis of Richard H. Thaler & Cass R. Sunstein's *Nudge: Improving Decisions about Health, Wealth, and Happiness*	解析理查德·H. 泰勒/卡斯·R. 桑斯坦《助推：如何做出有关健康、财富和幸福的更优决策》	心理学
An Analysis of Gordon Allport's *The Nature of Prejudice*	解析高尔登·奥尔波特《偏见的本质》	心理学
An Analysis of Steven Pinker's *The Better Angels of Our Nature: Why Violence Has Declined*	解析斯蒂芬·平克《人性中的善良天使：暴力为什么会减少》	心理学
An Analysis of Stanley Milgram's *Obedience to Authority*	解析斯坦利·米尔格拉姆《对权威的服从》	心理学
An Analysis of Betty Friedan's *The Feminine Mystique*	解析贝蒂·弗里丹《女性的奥秘》	心理学
An Analysis of David Riesman's *The Lonely Crowd: A Study of the Changing American Character*	解析大卫·理斯曼《孤独的人群：美国人社会性格演变之研究》	社会学
An Analysis of Franz Boas's *Race, Language and Culture*	解析弗朗兹·博厄斯《种族、语言与文化》	社会学
An Analysis of Pierre Bourdieu's *Outline of a Theory of Practice*	解析皮埃尔·布尔迪厄《实践理论大纲》	社会学
An Analysis of Max Weber's *The Protestant Ethic and the Spirit of Capitalism*	解析马克斯·韦伯《新教伦理与资本主义精神》	社会学
An Analysis of Jane Jacobs's *The Death and Life of Great American Cities*	解析简·雅各布斯《美国大城市的死与生》	社会学
An Analysis of C. Wright Mills's *The Sociological Imagination*	解析C. 赖特·米尔斯《社会学的想象力》	社会学
An Analysis of Robert E. Lucas Jr.'s *Why Doesn't Capital Flow from Rich to Poor Countries?*	解析小罗伯特·E. 卢卡斯《为何资本不从富国流向穷国？》	社会学

An Analysis of Émile Durkheim's *On Suicide*	解析埃米尔·迪尔凯姆《自杀论》	社会学
An Analysis of Eric Hoffer's *The True Believer: Thoughts on the Nature of Mass Movements*	解析埃里克·霍弗《狂热分子：群众运动圣经》	社会学
An Analysis of Jared M. Diamond's *Collapse: How Societies Choose to Fail or Survive*	解析贾雷德·M.戴蒙德《大崩溃：社会如何选择兴亡》	社会学
An Analysis of Michel Foucault's *The History of Sexuality Vol. 1: The Will to Knowledge*	解析米歇尔·福柯《性史（第一卷）：求知意志》	社会学
An Analysis of Michel Foucault's *Discipline and Punish*	解析米歇尔·福柯《规训与惩罚》	社会学
An Analysis of Richard Dawkins's *The Selfish Gene*	解析理查德·道金斯《自私的基因》	社会学
An Analysis of Antonio Gramsci's *Prison Notebooks*	解析安东尼奥·葛兰西《狱中札记》	社会学
An Analysis of Augustine's *Confessions*	解析奥古斯丁《忏悔录》	神学
An Analysis of C. S. Lewis's *The Abolition of Man*	解析C.S.路易斯《人之废》	神学

图书在版编目（CIP）数据

解析约翰·A.霍布森《帝国主义》/ 赖利·奎恩（Riley Quinn）著；黄辉辉译. —上海：上海外语教育出版社，2021
（世界思想宝库钥匙丛书）
ISBN 978-7-5446-6731-9

Ⅰ.①解… Ⅱ.①赖…②黄… Ⅲ.①帝国主义－研究 Ⅳ.①F038

中国版本图书馆CIP数据核字（2021）第033007号

This Chinese-English bilingual edition of *An Analysis of J. A. Hobson's Imperialism: A Study* is published by arrangement with MACAT International Limited.
Licensed for sale throughout the world.

本书汉英双语版由Macat国际有限公司授权上海外语教育出版社有限公司出版。
供在全世界范围内发行、销售。

图字：09 – 2018 – 549

出版发行：**上海外语教育出版社**
（上海外国语大学内） 邮编：200083
电　　话：021-65425300（总机）
电子邮箱：bookinfo@sflep.com.cn
网　　址：http://www.sflep.com
责任编辑：梁瀚杰

印　　刷：上海信老印刷厂
开　　本：890×1240　1/32　印张 5.875　字数 120千字
版　　次：2021年6月第1版　2021年6月第1次印刷
书　　号：ISBN 978-7-5446-6731-9
定　　价：30.00 元

本版图书如有印装质量问题，可向本社调换
质量服务热线：4008-213-263　电子邮箱：**editorial@sflep.com**